FRIENDS WITH GOD

BIBLE LESSONS

13 Surprising Visitors Bring Bible Lessons to Life

Group

Real. Bold. Love.

Loveland, Colorado

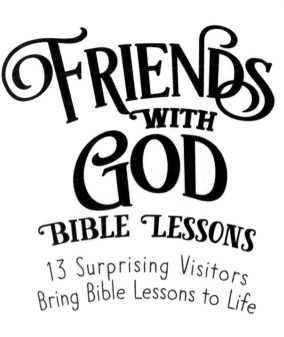

FRIENDS WITH GOD
BIBLE LESSONS
13 Surprising Visitors Bring Bible Lessons to Life

Copyright © 2019 Group Publishing, Inc./ 0000 0001 0362 4853

Visit our website: **group.com**

Credits
Contributing Authors: Jess Goldsmith, Jan Kershner, Laycie McClain, Jennifer Sundin, and Jeff White
Chief Creative Officer: Joani Schultz
Editor: Jody Brolsma
Assistant Editors: Lyndsay Gerwing and Becky Helzer
Cover Designer: Stephen Caine
Interior Designer: Darrin Stoll
Illustrator: David Harrington

Scripture quotations are taken from the Holy Bible, New Living Translation, copyright ©1996, 2004, 2007, 2013, 2015 by Tyndale House Foundation. Used by permission of Tyndale House Publishers, Inc., Carol Stream, Illinois 60188. All rights reserved.

"Made for This" by Jay Stocker. © 2017 Group Publishing, Inc. All rights reserved. No unauthorized use or duplication permitted.

"We Can Trust Him" (Psalm 33:4) by Jay Stocker. © 2007, 2009 Group Publishing, Inc. All rights reserved. No unauthorized use or duplication permitted.

"God Is Listening" by Jay Stocker. © 2011 Group Publishing, Inc. All rights reserved. No unauthorized use or duplication permitted.

"God Will Guide Us" by Jay Stocker. © 2014 Group Publishing, Inc. All rights reserved. No unauthorized use or duplication permitted.

"All Creatures of Our God and King" words by St. Francis of Assisi; English translation by William H. Draper. Arrangement © 2014 Group Publishing, Inc. All rights reserved. No unauthorized use or duplication permitted.

"I Will Not Be Afraid" by Jay Stocker. © 2009, 2019 Group Publishing, Inc. All rights reserved. No unauthorized use or duplication permitted.

"Your Friend" by Jay Stocker. © 2005 Group Publishing, Inc. All rights reserved. No unauthorized use or duplication permitted.

"God Is for Me" by Jay Stocker. © 2017 Group Publishing, Inc. All rights reserved. No unauthorized use or duplication permitted.

"My God Is Powerful" by Jay Stocker. © 2015 Group Publishing, Inc. All rights reserved. No unauthorized use or duplication permitted.
To download or stream more songs for your family, search for "GroupMusic" (one word, no quotes) on iTunes, Amazon or most music streaming sites.

"Pray About Everything" (Philippians 4:6-7) by Rob Biagi. © 2004, 2013 Group Publishing, Inc. All rights reserved. No unauthorized use or duplication permitted.

"God Loves Us So" by Jay Stocker. © 2014 Group Publishing, Inc. All rights reserved. No unauthorized use or duplication permitted.

"Through It All" by Jay Stocker. © 2012 Group Publishing, Inc. All rights reserved. No unauthorized use or duplication permitted.

ISBN: 978-1-4707-6007-6
Printed in the United States of America.

10 9 8 7 6 5 4 3 2 1   28 27 26 25 24 23 22 21 20 19

COMPANY'S COMING!

Imagine what it would be like to have Abram himself drop in and share about the night God showed him a sky full of stars and made a life-changing promise.

Or picture Moses delving into his adventures and bringing kids along to Egypt, the Red Sea, and freedom!

And if Naomi visited your classroom, how powerful would *her* story be, drawing kids into an epic journey with Ruth?

Well, *that's* just how real, surprising, and memorable your ministry is about to become! Each of these hour-long lessons includes an interactive script in which a Bible character drops in on your classroom to share his or her incredible, *true* adventures—and bring kids along for the ride. Each of these biblical accounts is told in the first person, inspired by the delightful *Friends With God Story Bible*. As kids explore the Bible story along with "the source," they'll discover that these action-packed, emotion-filled stories *actually* happened to *real* people.

All you need is a hammy volunteer who can look over the script and be familiar with it—and be willing to have fun with the role. You'll be on hand to distribute props and lead kids in joining the Bible adventure with all their senses. Oh, and of course each lesson includes friend-making icebreakers, giggle-inducing games, creative crafts, and powerful prayer times to reach every kind of learner.

But, hey, company's coming! Sweep the floor and get ready to open the door to a whole new way to bring the Bible to life!

...And for Kids and Families

These surprising friends of God can visit homes, too! Check out these incredible, family-friendly, faith-building resources for kids and families.

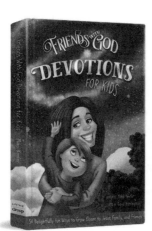

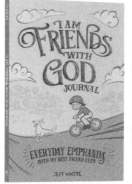

You're about to have 13 surprising visitors come to your Sunday school class...and change the way kids look at the Bible!

Contents

BIBLE STORY: **God creates Adam and Eve.** *(Genesis 1–2:24)*

BIBLE POINT: **God made you.**

BIBLE VERSE: **"Thank you for making me so wonderfully complex! Your workmanship is marvelous—how well I know it"** *(Psalm 139:14).*

Bible Insight

▸ In Genesis 1:26, God speaks of himself in the plural form when he says "Let us make human beings in our image." This is often thought of as a reference to the Trinity, as well as an acknowledgment of God's majesty. However, you may not know that throughout history, kings traditionally used plurals when referring to themselves. This "royal we" is known to have occurred in the Hebrew language and fits with the idea of the Trinity.

▸ Genesis isn't the only book that gives us the image of people made from dust or clay. Job 4:19 and many passages throughout Psalms refer to people being created from earth. Not only did God shape and form us from dust, but he breathed his own breath into our lungs to give us life!

▸ It's interesting to note that after God created human beings on the sixth day, he looked at all he had made and saw that it was *very* good—not just good.

▸ Scholars have found that ancient Near Eastern literature appears to be devoid of any narrative relating to the creation of woman. Only the Bible shares the unique account of God making woman.

Kid Insight

Do you remember dreaming when you were a kid about what you might be when you grew up? It's likely that over the years you explored possibilities and changed your mind as you discovered your gifts and abilities. Yet today's kids are under intense pressure to excel, specialize, and succeed—even as young children! Our culture is quick to label kids, and when kids haven't yet discovered their gifts, they often struggle with feelings of inadequacy. Use this lesson to celebrate the magnificent, marvelous, and even mysterious way God created each of us! You'll remind kids that they're crafted by God's hands and designed *exactly* the way he wants them to be.

You'll need:

- ☐ kid-friendly Bible
- ☐ photocopies of the "Buddy Bingo" cards (1 per child, p. 15)
- ☐ pens or pencils (1 per child)
- ☐ volunteer to play Adam
- ☐ Bible-times costume for Adam
- ☐ spray bottle of water, set to "mist"
- ☐ brown modeling dough (small handful per child)
- ☐ variety of craft items such as pompoms, wiggly eyes, cardboard tubes, chenille wires, and construction paper
- ☐ glue
- ☐ washable ink pads
- ☐ index cards (1 per child)
- ☐ wet wipes (1 per child)
- ☐ *Friends With God Bible Lessons Music* CD and music player

---

If you can't find a volunteer to play Adam, modify your script slightly and play the role yourself. You'll simply need to have kids close their eyes and put on their imaginations while *you* don the Bible-times costume. If you're female, tweak the script and play this as Eve.

Getting Ready

Make a sample Creative Critter to use as your example.

~❋ THE LESSON ❋~

Friend-Maker Icebreaker (*10 minutes*)

BUDDY BINGO

Welcome kids and introduce yourself.

Say: **When we get together here at** [name of your church], **you're surrounded by friends. But I'll bet you have lots of people you like to hang out with *outside* this building, too. That makes me wonder something!** Ask:

💬 **Tell about your closest friend and why you like to spend time with that person.**

Give your own example first, sharing about a friend or family member you like to spend time with and why. Then let kids share with people sitting near them.

Say: **There are probably friends here you know really well and some you've never met before. This game will give you a chance to get to know each other a little better.**

Hand each child a Buddy Bingo card and a pen or pencil. Explain that kids will have about five minutes to see how well they can fill up their cards with signatures. Tell kids that when they find someone in the room who matches a description on the card, that person will sign his or her name in that box. Tell kids their goal is to get as many different signatures as they can to fill up their cards (but people *can* sign twice if they meet more than one description).

Have kids begin by filling in something unique about themselves in the "Free Space!" and then signing their names in that spot.

Play "Made for This" from the *Friends With God Bible Lessons Music* CD for about five minutes, allowing kids to interact, get to know each other, and gather signatures. After five minutes, turn off the music and have kids sit down. Ask:

💬 **What did you learn about your friends?**

💬 **What was the most surprising thing you learned?**

💬 **How is this like or unlike the way you get to know friends in real life?**

Say: **One friend who's with us here today—and every day—is God. You may not think of God as your friend, but the Bible tells us that God calls us his friend! Wow! Today we'll get to know someone else in the Bible who was a friend of God. In fact, you might say he was God's first friend!**

Set the cards and pens aside for the next activity.

MEET ADAM

Place the modeling dough where "Adam" can reach it. Adam should enter and begin a dialogue with kids. You may be needed to assist Adam with props or lighting. Join in the fun and surprise of talking with this friend of God!

(Enter and begin enthusiastically.)

Wow! I mean, WOW! *(Look around at all the kids with joy and excitement.)* **Look at all of you INCREDIBLE creations!**

(Walk among the kids, commenting on God's creativity in how he made each one. Have fun noting kids' cool eye colors, hair textures, limbs, and even freckles!)

Aren't people AMAZING? My name is Adam. God gave me that name himself. *Ask:*

💬 **Who gave you your name?** *(Let a few kids share their responses with the group, then continue.)*

I have to tell you what's been happening to me. You see, it all started with God. He's been REALLY busy the last few days. First there was nothing. Shout out your very favorite thing that God made. *(Pause and let kids call out their favorite creations.)*

Well, none of that existed! It was a little like this. *(Have the leader dim the lights.)* **Then every day God made something new. Light** *(have the leader turn the lights back up)*, **the ocean** *(have the leader mist kids with a spray bottle)*, **the sky, the sun and moon, plants, trees, flowers, fish, birds—you name it. Everything was made for a reason, and it was good.** *(Lead kids in giving a thumbs-up sign to show that those things are good.)*

Yesterday God made these things called animals. They're wonderful creatures! *(Look closely at the kids.)* **Some of you remind me of those animals. Maybe you can act like YOUR favorite animal.** *(Pause while kids act like different animals. Guess which animals kids are acting out.)*

God made big ones and small ones. Furry ones and tough ones. Spotted ones and striped ones. Some have long necks, and others have sharp teeth. Each one is unique. God is so creative!

And then God made something extra special. God made ME. *(Stick out your chest proudly.)* **God took some dirt from the ground—the freshest dirt you've ever seen—and shaped me into the first-ever, brand-new, pleased-to-meet-you human being! THAT'S something only God can do. Let me show you what I mean.**

(Have the leader help you hand out a small handful of brown modeling dough to each child. Give kids a couple of minutes to each sculpt a person from their dough. Comment on the different ways kids make their people.)

Then God breathed the breath of life into me! Wow! How does that work with the creations YOU made? *(Let kids breathe on their creations.)* *Ask:*

💬 **Why didn't your creations come to life?**

Only God has such awesome, creative power to create LIFE! Wow. *(Have kids set their creations against one wall.)*

God's world is awesome. But God wasn't done after he made me. There was something even better coming along! First, God made me go to sleep. Then God took one of my ribs *(touch your side)* **and turned it into the most dazzling creature I've ever seen: a woman! God named her Eve...and she's beautiful! Now she's my wife. We watch over the animals and take care of the garden we live in—the Garden of Eden—together. God has given us everything we need.**

God must REALLY love us.

(Look closely at the kids again.)

<u>God made each and every one of YOU</u> with his very own hands. When God made people, he said THAT creation was VERY GOOD!

(Have kids join you in giving two thumbs up to show that people were called "very good." Then show off some of the "very good" things you've discovered you can do, such as clap your hands, jump up and down, and dance in a silly way.) Ask:

 **What are some "very good" things YOU can do?** *(Let kids each demonstrate things such as snapping, crossing their eyes, skipping, and standing on their hands. Applaud after each "very good" thing.)*

God CHOSE to make you! God wanted you to be a part of our very special world. <u>God made you</u> exactly as you are, and God never makes mistakes. And you know the best part? God made us because he loves us so much. And God will never stop loving us. Isn't that amazing?

Well, I need to go. It's my job to feed the giraffes today, and I don't want to miss that!

(Wave goodbye and exit.)

"That's Me" Tag

Say: **When <u>God made you</u>, he used the same care, creativity, and attention he used when he made Adam and Eve!** Let's play a game to keep getting to know each other and celebrate the way God made each person here.

Listen as I call out a description. For example, I might call out, "You have green eyes." If that's true of you, you'll hold up a hand and keep it up as you run! Everyone else—people whose eyes are *not* green—will be "It" and will try to tag you. If you get tagged, freeze until I call out the next description. Got it?

Call out the following descriptions and have kids play along:

- ▸ **Your favorite food is pizza.**
- ▸ **You have brown eyes.**
- ▸ **You can touch your tongue to your nose.**
- ▸ **You play on a sports team.**
- ▸ **You have blond hair.**
- ▸ **You have braces.**
- ▸ **You like to dance.**
- ▸ **You haven't been tagged yet!**

If you don't have a large room, kids can take giant steps rather than run. Choose a few kids to call out descriptions if they have some creative suggestions. Then gather kids together. Ask:

💬 **How did you feel when I called out something that described you?**

💬 **In real life, do you ever wish God made you differently? Why?**

Since this is a more personal question, be sure to share your own example. You might share that you sometimes wish you were taller or better at sports so you could play with your kids. Then let kids share with a few friends seated nearby. After a minute or two, take a few responses from anyone willing to share with the larger group.

Say: **In the Bible, a guy named David *celebrated* the way God made him. Listen to this!** Read aloud Psalm 139:14 from a kid-friendly Bible translation. Ask:

💬 **How do you feel when you hear these words?**

💬 **Why is it sometimes hard to remember that we're God's workmanship—something he lovingly created?**

Say: **<u>God made you</u>! And the Bible says that as something God made, you're marvelous and complex. That means you're detailed and complicated and wonderful! Wow, you!**

CREATIVE CRITTERS

Set out a variety of craft supplies (this is a great time to clean out your craft closet!). Include things like pompoms, wiggly eyes, chenille wires, cardboard tubes, construction paper, and glue.

Let kids craft and create their own unique animals using the supplies you've provided. Kids can make models of real animals, combinations of animals, or their own unique creations. While kids work, point out how *our* creativity comes from God because we were made in God's image with some of his characteristics. Let kids share any fun facts they know about animals or about creation.

After eight minutes, have kids clean up and then set their animal creations near their clay creations from the Bible Adventure. Celebrate the fact that **God made us** and the amazing world in which we live.

THUMB-THING SPECIAL

Form a circle and have kids sit down.

Say: **Each person is crafted and created by God. God made you *exactly* the way he wants you to be—inside and out. Sometimes we don't feel very special. We feel ordinary. Or worse, we feel *less* than ordinary! But you carry something with you to remind you of just how unique and special you are.**

Set out ink pads, and give each person an index card. Have kids form pairs where they're seated. Direct each child to make a fingerprint on his or her card. Have partners compare their fingerprints to see how different they are.

Say: **Did you know that you got your fingerprints while you were still in your mom's tummy? Even before you were born! The fluid that surrounds a baby before it's born swirls by the baby's fresh skin and leaves these marks. How awesome is that? The Bible book of Psalms says to God, "Thank you for making me so wonderfully complex! Your workmanship is marvelous—how well I know it." Let's use our fingerprints as we talk to God.**

Pray: **God, thank you for loving us and creating us. We can't imagine how much you love us. Sometimes the world around us makes us feel not-so-marvelous. We don't feel wonderful. Listen as we silently tell you the times we feel hurt, small, or not special.**

Have kids silently pray as they each make a thumbprint on their cards.

Continue praying: **God, thanks for making us in your image. *You* breathed life into us. When we feel sad or unimportant, help us remember that we were lovingly created by your hands. Speak a word of love or comfort to our hearts right now.**

Have kids listen and rest in God's peace as they make a second thumbprint, overlapping the bottom of the first one to make a heart.

Close your prayer: **God, thank you for loving us enough to make us so wonderfully complex. In Jesus' name, amen.**

Distribute wet wipes so kids can clean the ink from their fingers. Let kids take their index cards home as a reminder that they were lovingly crafted by God's hands.

Buddy Bingo

Ask around to see who matches these descriptions.

I'm the oldest kid in my family.	I can do a cartwheel.	I wear glasses.	I can play an instrument.	I can do a handstand.
I have freckles.	I love reading.	I've lived in the same house my whole life.	I don't drink milk.	I baked something in the past week.
I can speak a different language.	I can blow a bubble with gum.	**Free Space!** I can…	I have curly hair.	I've been in a play.
I have a birthday in March.	I do *not* know how to whistle.	I've broken a bone.	I'm left-handed.	I'm a twin.
I'm afraid of the dark.	I've moved more than three times.	I ride my bike to school.	I want to be a singer.	I've had a lemonade stand.

Stars In My Eyes

BIBLE STORY: **God makes a promise to Abram.** *(Genesis 15)*

BIBLE POINT: <u>**God keeps his promises.**</u>

BIBLE VERSE: **"Understand, therefore, that the Lord your God is indeed God. He is the faithful God who keeps his covenant for a thousand generations and lavishes his unfailing love on those who love and obey his commands"** *(Deuteronomy 7:9).*

Bible Insight

▸ It's interesting to note that just before God made this promise to Abram, Abram had fought a battle to protect his cousin, Lot. After the battle, the king of Sodom offered Abram a reward, but knowing the king of Sodom would use the reward against him, Abram refused. What Abram didn't know at this point was that God would reward him with something far better—a promise of land and many descendants. The king of Sodom's reward was nothing compared to what God could promise!

▸ A foreshadowing of Jesus' sacrifice for us, God's promises aren't based on our sin, doubt, or attitudes. Despite Abram's self-pitying attitude ("Since you've given me no children, Eliezer of Damascus, a servant in my household, will inherit all my wealth," Abram said to God), when God approaches him with a promise, God's plan and his lavish love for Abram don't change. He kindly shares his promise with Abram. And then Abram believes right away—which is counted as righteousness!

▸ God always keeps his promises to us, but a promise doesn't guarantee immediate fulfillment, as we often expect. Abram waited 15 years for God to fulfill this promise, and we can continue to wait and trust God's promises, no matter how long it feels like they're taking.

Kid Insight

Kids experience deep disappointments and fear just as adults do. Whether their parents are on the verge of divorce, their families are moving to a new city or state, or they fail in a competition or sport that they'd put their all into, it's not unnatural for kids to feel disheartened. Yet kids can find hope as they discover that Abram experienced discouragement and God came alongside him, promising future blessings. As they find out that God is faithful and always keeps his promises, children will learn to put their trust in him and wait for God to carry out his plans in *their* lives.

You'll need:

- ☐ kid-friendly Bible
- ☐ paper slips (1 per child)
- ☐ pencils
- ☐ basket
- ☐ volunteer to play Abram
- ☐ Bible-times costume for Abram
- ☐ glow-in-the-dark star stickers (1 per child, plus 10 extra)
- ☐ balloons in 2 colors (1 balloon per child)
- ☐ 2 large plastic bags for holding inflated balloons
- ☐ *Friends With God Bible Lessons Music* CD and music player
- ☐ timer
- ☐ wooden coffee stirrers (5 per child, plus 5 for your sample)
- ☐ tacky glue
- ☐ fine-tipped markers
- ☐ tissue paper
- ☐ needle
- ☐ fishing line (about 1 foot per child)

If you can't find a volunteer to play Abram, modify your script slightly and play the role yourself. You'll simply need to have kids close their eyes and put on their imaginations while *you* don the Bible-times costume. If you're female, tweak the script and play this as Sarai, sharing what she heard from Abram about what happened.

Getting Ready

"Charge" the glow stickers by putting them near a light source. Keep them near the light as long as possible so they'll glow brightly when you use them during the lesson.

Inflate one balloon per child, making half of the balloons one color and half another color. (If you have mostly older kids in class, they may be able to inflate and tie off their own balloons during the "Don't Let 'Em Down" game.) Put the balloons, sorted by color, into large plastic bags.

Make a sample Promise Star to use as your example.

✥ THE LESSON ✥

Friend-Maker Icebreaker *(10 minutes)*

MATCH THE PROMISE TO THE PERSON

Welcome kids and introduce yourself.

Say: **Promises are an important part of friendship. When we say we'll do something, our friends rely on us to keep our word. Keeping our promises with one another helps us have strong friendships.** Ask:

💬 **Tell about a promise you made to a friend, or one the two of you made together.**

Give your own example first, sharing about a promise you've made. Then let kids share with people sitting near them.

Say: **We all make promises to our friends and families. Let's make some fun promises with our friends here at church. When I give you a slip of paper, write down something unique or special you can do. By writing it down, you're guaranteeing that you can really do it.** Give a few examples to get kids thinking. Kids might say they can tread water for five minutes without stopping, they can open a candy wrapper without using their hands, they can recite the first 20 numbers in pi, or they can do three cartwheels in a row.

Give each child a slip of paper and a pencil. Say: **On the paper, write "I promise that I can…" and then write what you can do. Keep your promise a secret, because we'll be guessing who can do what in a moment.** Allow a couple of minutes for kids to write their promises and then put them in a basket.

One at a time, invite kids to pull out a slip and read it aloud. Invite the class to venture two guesses as to who the promise belongs to. If time and logistics allow, kids can perform their promises.

After all the promises have been guessed, ask:

💬 **Whose promise surprised you the most?**

💬 **Were any of the promises hard to believe? If so, why?**

💬 **Why is it important to you that your friends keep their promises?**

Say: **We have a friend here today who always, always, always does what he says—God. Sometimes God's promises might be so amazing that they're hard to believe. But** God *always* keeps his promises. **Today we'll hear about an amazing promise God made to another one of his friends, named Abram.** Place the pencils, slips of paper, and basket aside.

Meet Abram

Place the star stickers where "Abram" can reach them. Abram should enter and begin a dialogue with kids. You may be needed to assist Abram with props or lighting. Join in the fun and surprise of talking with this friend of God!

(Enter and begin enthusiastically.)

There are promises *(hold your hands out in front of you as if you're holding a soccer ball)*, **and then there are PROMISES.** *(Stretch your arms out wide.)*

God made ME *(point to yourself)* **a promise that was so hard to believe that I just HAD to believe it.** *Ask:*

💬 **What's the biggest, most important thing someone has ever told YOU they'd do?**
(Take and respond to several kids' examples, and then move on.)

Those are pretty big promises—but let me tell you about the big promise God made to me. It started when I was feeling sorry for myself. I looked like this: *(Stick out your lower lip as if you're pouting.)*

Let's see your pity-party faces. *(Walk among kids, pointing out kids who are making unique pity-party faces. Have the ones you think are the top three get up with you in front of the rest of the kids. Have kids vote on which face they think is the poutiest.)*

I was having a pity party, even though God had blessed me with riches and a long life. I'd won battles and made a lot of friends. God had even protected me more times than I could count. There were a lot of good things about my life! Tell someone next to you something you're thankful for about your life. Go! *(Walk among kids, listening. After about a minute, share several things kids said they were thankful for.)*

We all have something to be thankful for. But even so, I was still sad. I was sad because God hadn't given me and my wife, Sarai, any children. Right now, shout out the name of every child in your family: brothers, sisters, cousins, and so on. *(Pause and let kids call out names.)*

See! You're surrounded by kids, kids, and more kids. But Sarai and I weren't. How could God bless me with so much, yet not give me a family to share with my wife?

(Pause and smile.) **You know what God did? God made me a promise.**

First God took me outside. It was dark out. *(Have the leader turn out the lights.)* **God showed me the stars in the vast night sky.** *(Reach up as high as you can and begin placing the charged glow-in-the-dark stickers on the wall or ceiling. Place only about 10 of them.)*

"How many stars do you see?" God asked me. *(Invite kids to each take a turn placing a sticker as high up as they can reach. Lead them in counting the stars after they're all placed.)*

Okay, there aren't as many stars here as there are in the sky. Take a guess—how many stars do you think there are in the REAL sky? *(Pause as kids call out numbers.)*

There are too many stars to count in the real sky. I told God that. And God said, "That's how many descendants you will have." *(Pause and smile.)* **"That's a promise," he told me!**

"Wow," I thought. That many generations from me? That's a pretty big family...a HUGE family! Give me a thumbs-up if your family is as big as THAT—as many as the stars in the sky. *(Pause and look around.)* **No one?**

That was kind of an unbelievable promise, right? *(Look around at kids for a response.)*

Unbelievable or not, I knew God loved me, so I believed him.

But God didn't stop there.

"Your family will need a place to live, so I'm giving you all the land you see before you," God said. *(Point around the room.)* **Again, WOW. This was some GOOD land!** *Ask:*

💬 **What new place would you want God to give you?** *(Take several kids' answers and then move on.)*

You never know what God might promise YOU. One thing's for sure: I'll never look at the stars the same way again. *(Look up at the star stickers on your ceiling as if you're pondering God's promise again.)*

Well, God kept his promise...which means I have to get back to my HUGE family. Even though there are a bunch of them, they sure miss me when I'm gone!

(Wave goodbye and exit.)

DON'T LET 'EM DOWN

Say: **Abram discovered that** <u>God keeps his promises</u>. **That didn't happen only in the Bible!** <u>God keeps his promises</u> **to us, too. That means we can always count on him to do what he says. God won't let us down. Let's play a game where we don't let balloons down. We'll gently bop them in the air and try to keep them from touching the ground. We'll start with one minute, and after some practice, we'll try to keep the balloons up for an entire song!**

Form two equal teams. Assign each team a balloon color, and give each child a balloon. Explain that kids will try to keep their team's balloons up. Have teams gather and mix up randomly—this will make the game more of a challenge.

Count to three, and have kids all toss their balloons in the air. Turn on the *Friends With God Bible Lessons Music* CD to the song "We Can Trust Him" (Psalm 33:4). Set the timer for one minute. As soon as one balloon touches the floor, stop the music and announce the time. If kids keep their balloons up for a full minute, increase the time *and* add on a limitation for hitting the balloons—for example, kids can't use their right hand, can't move their feet, or can use only one index finger. Challenge kids to meet a longer time period until they're able to keep all the balloons up for a full song, or as time allows.

Collect all the balloons. Ask:

💬 **In the game, I kept making it harder for you to keep the balloons up. In real life, what things make it hard to keep up with your promises?**

Give kids time to think by giving your own example, such as getting too busy, forgetting that you made a promise, or making too many promises to too many people.

💬 **How does it feel to know that** <u>God always keeps his promises</u> **and** *never* **lets us down?**

Say: **We have friends and family members who make promises, but sometimes they get busy, forget, or can't come through for us. God is mighty, powerful, and perfect. We can be sure that he'll never let us down. The Bible tells us why. Listen to this.** Read Deuteronomy 7:9. Ask:

💬 **What does this verse tell us about why we can trust God?**

Say: **People might have trouble keeping their promises, but God never does. He's our faithful God! He promised to bless Abram with a huge family and plenty of land to live on. The verse we just read tells us that God promises to take care of** *us*, **too. And we can count on him to not let us down, because** <u>God keeps his promises</u>!

PROMISE STARS

Say: **God told Abram to look in the sky. That was God's way of showing Abram that he was promising to give him countless kids, grandkids, and great-grandkids—a huge family! And God did! <u>God keeps his promises</u> to us, too. The Bible is filled with God's promises to always love us, forgive us, and care for us. Let's make stars to help us remember God's promises.**

Give each child five wooden coffee stirrers, and set out tacky glue, fine-tipped markers, and tissue paper. Show kids how to glue the ends of the coffee stirrers together one at a time until they complete a star.

While the glue dries, talk about some promises God makes to us. Have kids write a few of the following promises on their stars (it's okay if kids write only a few words of the promise):

- ▸ **God promises to love us.**
- ▸ **God promises to forgive us because of Jesus.**
- ▸ **God promises to give us what we need.**
- ▸ **God promises to listen to us.**
- ▸ **God promises to always be with us.**
- ▸ **God promises we can be with him in heaven because of Jesus.**

As you share each promise, have kids tear a piece of tissue paper to fit one section of the star. Then have kids glue the tissue paper to the wooden frame. By the time they've finished, kids' stars will look like stained glass.

Say: **<u>God keeps his promises</u>, and these Promise Stars can remind us of that!** Use a needle to thread some fishing line through one tip of each child's star. Have kids tie a loop so they can hang their stars in front of a window.

PROMISE PRAYERS

Say: **When God made a promise to Abram, Abram believed it even though God's promise was so amazing that it *seemed* unbelievable. God kept his promise to Abram, and** <u>God keeps his promises</u> **to us, too.**

Hold up a Promise Star. **These stars remind us of some promises that God has made to you and me. Some might be hard for you to believe, and others might be easier. Let's talk to God about these promises. You might ask God to help you believe. You might thank God because you've already seen God keep a promise to you. You can talk honestly with God about each promise.**

Lead kids through the promises on the Promise Star. Have them touch each promise as you name it, and give them about a minute per promise to talk to God silently.

▸ **God promises to love us.**

▸ **God promises to forgive us because of Jesus.**

▸ **God promises to give us what we need.**

▸ **God promises to listen to us.**

▸ **God promises to always be with us.**

▸ **God promises we can be with him in heaven because of Jesus.**

Close in prayer, and then say: **God will keep these promises to you, and as you grow closer to your friend God, you may find that he makes other promises to you, too. You can always trust God. You can expect amazing things like Abram did, because** <u>God keeps his promises</u>**.**

BETTER SAFE THAN SORRY

BIBLE STORY: **Moses receives the Ten Commandments.** *(Exodus 20:1-21)*

BIBLE POINT: **God guides us.**

BIBLE VERSE: **"My father taught me, 'Take my words to heart. Follow my commands, and you will live' "** *(Proverbs 4:4)*.

Bible Insight

▸ In Matthew 22, the religious leaders asked about the *greatest* commandment. Jesus' response may summarize the heart of the Ten Commandments: " 'You must love the Lord your God with all your heart, all your soul, and all your mind.' This is the first and greatest commandment. A second is equally important: 'Love your neighbor as yourself.' " The first four commandments focus on our relationship with God, while the other six direct our relationships with other people.

▸ Have you ever heard the argument that the Ten Commandments don't apply to Christians? Proponents of this argument quote Romans 6:14: "Sin is no longer your master, for you no longer live under the requirements of the law. Instead, you live under the freedom of God's grace." However, out of context this verse can be misused. Paul continues on to say that we now "wholeheartedly obey [God's] teaching" (Romans 6:17). And in Matthew 5:17, Jesus says, "Don't misunderstand why I have come. I did not come to abolish the law of Moses or the writings of the prophets. No, I came to accomplish their purpose." The Ten Commandments are a guide for God's friends to live the way God designed.

▸ Some scholars believe that the Ten Commandments are a summary of the full law—that they're more like an outline of the core messages of the lengthy Law of Moses, rather than being separate law.

▸ The Ten Commandments weren't necessarily new to the Israelite population. Each of the commandments is mentioned in Genesis; therefore, the Ten Commandments may have been only the formal presentation of them.

Kid Insight

Most kids have plenty of rules they're expected to follow. Their parents have rules. At school, their teachers inform them of the rules they must follow—and they probably have different sets of rules in the music room, gym, computer lab, and homeroom. There are rules for sports teams, the community pool, and even Sunday school. These rules are made with good intentions. However, kids shouldn't think of God's commandments as just another set of rules they have to follow. Help kids understand that God's commandments are designed to guide us through life, helping us live lives that are healthy, joyful, and honoring to God. Today, guide kids as they discover that the Ten Commandments were made out of God's pure loving care and desire to *guide* kids to the best life possible.

You'll need:

- ☐ kid-friendly Bible
- ☐ volunteer to play Moses
- ☐ Bible-times clothes for Moses
- ☐ red crepe paper strips (1 yard per child)
- ☐ notebook
- ☐ wet wipes for cleaning hands
- ☐ unsweetened rice or corn cereal, such as Chex (¼ cup per child)
- ☐ chocolate chips (about 1 tablespoon per child)
- ☐ raisins (about 1 tablespoon per child)
- ☐ mini pretzels (about ¼ cup per child)
- ☐ ¼-cup measuring cups (2)
- ☐ 1-cup measuring cups (2)
- ☐ gallon-size resealable plastic bags (1 for every group of 4 kids)
- ☐ 4 large bowls
- ☐ small cups (1 per child)
- ☐ craft supplies such as crayons, stickers, and colored tape
- ☐ paper (3 sheets per child)
- ☐ markers
- ☐ stapler (1 for every 10 kids)
- ☐ *Friends With God Bible Lessons Music* CD and music player

---

If you can't find a volunteer to play Moses, modify your script slightly and play the role yourself. You'll simply need to have kids close their eyes and put on their imaginations while *you* don the Bible-times costume. If you're female, tweak the script and play this as an Israelite friend of Moses', sharing what she heard from Moses about what happened.

Getting Ready

Put each of the snack ingredients into its own large bowl. Put 1-cup measuring cups in the bowls of mini pretzels and cereal, and put ¼-cup measuring cups in the bowls of chocolate chips and raisins. Set the bowls out of sight.

Friend-Maker Icebreaker *(10 minutes)*

TELL IT TOOTHLESS

Welcome kids and introduce yourself.

Say: **You've probably *heard* about the Ten Commandments, even if you don't know what they are. They're a set of do's and don'ts that our good friend God has given us to follow. You might call them "rules," which doesn't sound like something you'd get from a friend. But the Ten Commandments help us live the best lives! Because of that, we're going to start off with a game where we'll have a fun "rule" we'll have to follow.**

Have kids sit in a circle. Explain that kids will be "passing" questions around the circle. Begin by demonstrating.

Ask the child to your right a yes-or-no question, such as "Do you like the color blue?" or "Do you like pepperoni on your pizza?" Here's the rule: You can't show your teeth! Instead, use your lips to hide your teeth as you speak. (This looks and sounds very silly. The sillier, the better! When kids laugh, it's nearly impossible for them *not* to show their teeth.)

Tell the child next to you to answer without showing his or her teeth. Then that child will ask a different yes-or-no question to the person on his or her right. The goal is to ask and answer as quickly as possible so everyone around the circle gets to ask and answer a question. If someone shows his or her teeth, that person is out. Play one round, then begin a new round with this additional rule: You can ask the question to the person on your right *or* switch directions and ask the person on your left! After a couple of rounds, ask:

- 💬 **What did you think of the rule we had for our game?**
- 💬 **Why do you think I put that rule in the game?**
- 💬 **Call out some other rules you have to follow.**
- 💬 **Why do you think we have rules like that?**

Say: **In the Bible, God gave his friend Moses some important rules for us. Today we'll find out that God gave us those rules because we're his friends and he loves us more than we can imagine! God wants the very best for us, so those rules are one way <u>God guides us</u>. Let's discover how God's commandments are for our best.**

MEET MOSES

Place the notebook where "Moses" can reach it. Moses should enter and begin a dialogue with kids. You may be needed to assist Moses with props or lighting. Join in the fun and surprise of talking with this friend of God!

(Enter and begin enthusiastically.)

Thanks for letting me drop in. I heard a lot of laughing in here. This must be a fun place to be! My name is Moses, and I've been in some fun places...and some not-so-fun places. No doubt about it, I've lived through some incredible adventures. *Ask:*

💬 **Tell me about the most exciting adventure YOU'VE ever been on.** *(Take three or four answers and then move on.)*

Well, from the time I was born, I've faced things in my life that no one else in all of history has experienced. Every step of the way, through every breath and every day, God has been there guiding me.

When I was a baby, God guided my mom to put me in a basket in the river. I know that sounds like an odd thing to do to a baby, but it was the only way she could think of to keep me safe.

God knew what was best, because that's where the king's own daughter found me and plucked me out of the river to save my life. Pharaoh's daughter raised me from a baby—and she hired my mom to be a sort of nanny even though she didn't know that was my mom!

Now, that kind of thing could happen only because God was guiding my life. *(Pause, as if remembering.)* But one of the coolest times was when God spoke to me in a...wait, you have to get into this a little more. This was INCREDIBLE!

(Have the leader give each child a crepe paper strip.)

I mean, I'm just watching my sheep out in the desert... Hey, you guys look like you could do some pretty decent sheep impressions. *(Lead kids to get up and follow you around the room, acting like sheep.)*

And I walk by this bush and... *(Pretend to do a double-take.)* The bush was on fire! *(Have kids join together in a tight circle, waving their crepe paper strips to make a crackling fire. You'll need to continue loudly for a while to be heard over the crackling.)*

But this bush wasn't burning up... On fire, but not burning? *(Ask several kids if they're burning up from the fire.)* It didn't make sense until God talked to me through the burning bush. I mean, God can do anything, so he can make a bush not burn up, right? God gave me some guidance then. *(Have kids put their crepe paper strips in a pile, then have them sit down.)*

Then there was the time God guided me in just the right way to lead his people across a wide, deep sea. It was a little like this...and when I say "little," I mean it. The Red Sea is HUGE! But let me show you anyway. Maybe some of you can be the crazy, wild, massive, scary Red Sea.

(Form two groups. Have one group stand behind you as the Israelites and the other group stand in front of you as the Red Sea. Direct the Red Sea kids to wave their arms and make splashing noises.)

The sea was so big that there was no way ALL of God's people could get across. But God told me to raise my hand. That seemed like a strange thing to do, but... *(Raise your hand over the "Red Sea.")* With God's power, the water split in half, leaving a dry path for everyone to walk on! *(Lead "Israelite" kids through the parted sea. Then have everyone sit again.)* I'm glad I followed God's guidance then!

I guess learning to follow God's guiding hand helped me understand some of the other things he did. Once, God sent me up to the top of a mountain so he could talk with me. There he gave me 10 instructions to help us live good lives that please him and keep us from hurting God and each other. *(Open the notebook and pretend to be reading the following.)* These instructions are called the Ten Commandments, so show me the number with your fingers as I say them. *(Lead kids to show the number you're saying as you read the Ten Commandments.)*

1. I am your God, and your only God.

2. Do not make any false gods and worship them.

3. Do not misuse God's name.

4. Rest on the Sabbath, and keep the day holy.

5. Honor your parents.

6. Do not murder.

7. Stay true to your husband or wife.

8. Do not steal.

9. Do not lie.

10. Do not want what others have.

If God's people can follow these simple instructions, they'll live happier lives that please God. I'm telling you, God's guidance is something we'll want to follow!

(Hold a hand up to your ear as if you're listening.) I think God has some more guidance for me. I'm going to a quiet place so I can listen. Great meeting you!

(Wave goodbye and exit.)

SNACK ATTACK

Say: **Wow! Moses experienced God's guidance throughout his entire life!** <u>God guides us</u>, **too. Just imagining Moses' wild adventures made me hungry. I say we make a snack...while we play a game!** Distribute wet wipes and let kids clean their hands. Have kids get into groups of four, and ask each group to choose a Snack-maker. Have groups gather at one end of your room. Explain that the Snack-makers must close their eyes and keep them closed.

Give each Snack-maker a gallon-size resealable plastic bag. While Snack-makers' eyes are closed, quietly bring out the large bowls of snack items. Put one bowl in each corner of the room. Tell kids they'll need to guide their unseeing Snack-maker to the ingredients so he or she can add one measuring cup of each item into the bag. Group members can't do anything except guide by talking. (If you're worried about Snack-makers tipping over the bowls, have a volunteer hold each bowl of ingredients.)

Have kids begin. Play the song "God Will Guide Us" from the *Friends With God Bible Lessons Music* CD while they play. When they've all finished, let groups gather. Hand out small cups, and let each child scoop a cup of the snack mix from the group's bag. While kids enjoy the snack, discuss the experience. Ask:

💬 **Snack-makers, what was the hardest part of this activity?**

💬 **If you were giving guidance, what was hard for you?**

💬 **Snack-makers, what was the best guidance you got from your group?**

💬 **How is this activity like or unlike the way God guides us today?**

Say: **God's guidance shows us the best way to live. Another one of God's friends, named Solomon, believed that, too. Listen to this.** Read Proverbs 4:4. Ask:

💬 **Why do you think both Moses and Solomon say it's a good thing that** <u>God guides us</u>?

Say: **Our Snack-makers needed help to make the best snack possible. When** <u>God guides us</u>, **he helps us make good decisions that make our lives better.**

TRAVEL GUIDE

Set out the craft supplies, paper, markers, and staplers. Show kids how to line up three sheets of paper and fold them to make a booklet. Help them staple the folded edge to keep the booklet pages together.

Say: **You're an expert of your town and neighborhood, right?** Ask:

💬 **What are the best things to do in** [name of your community]?

💬 **What places would you tell people to avoid?**

Have kids make travel guides using all the craft supplies. Encourage them to have a front cover and to fill each page with drawings and pictures of places to go, things to do, restaurant recommendations, and other advice. Play the *Friends With God Bible Lessons Music* CD while kids work.

Say: **Your guides will be a huge help to visitors to** [name of your community]. **They'll know where to go, what to do, and even things to avoid!** Ask:

💬 **How is your guide like or unlike the Ten Commandments?**

Say: <u>God guides us</u> **because he wants us to know the best things to do and things to avoid so we can have the best life!** Encourage kids to give their travel guides to any visitors who stay at their houses in the future.

PRAYER TRAIN

Have kids form a train, each holding on to the shoulders of the person in front of them. Lead kids around the room in different directions and doing different things, such as kicking out a leg, stepping over something, and ducking under something. Do this for a couple of minutes.

Say: **When** <u>God guides us</u>**, it can be like a fun ride! God has amazing things for us, like he did for Moses. That's why we can look at God's commandments as good things instead of as an old set of rules.**

Continue to lead kids in the train, but this time it's a prayer train. You'll guide kids for a few seconds, asking God for guidance in a specific area (such as at school, on the sports field, with siblings, or with friends), and then you'll run to the back of the train. Each person will have a chance to guide the train for a few seconds and say a prayer for God's guidance in a particular area. Kids can say their prayers silently if they'd like and then move to the back of the train.

Continue as time allows. Then close the prayer.

Now You're Talking

BIBLE STORY: **God speaks to Balaam.** *(Numbers 22:21-41)*

BIBLE POINT: <u>**God surprises us.**</u>

BIBLE VERSE: **"For just as the heavens are higher than the earth, so my ways are higher than your ways and my thoughts higher than your thoughts"** *(Isaiah 55:9).*

Bible Insight

▸ Earlier in Numbers 22, we find out that Balaam was actually responding to a request from an enemy of God's people to curse the Israelites. Balaam wasn't one of God's people, and yet God still stopped him and gave him directions. In the end and at the direction of God, Balaam blessed the Israelites instead of cursing them. The way God directed Balaam is a good reminder that God can surprise us by using anyone to bless his people.

▸ It's interesting to note that donkeys are often viewed as "dumb" animals, yet in this Bible story, it's the donkey who knows what's going on and the human who can't figure it out!

▸ The story of Balaam and his donkey may seem like an isolated story, but it's actually mentioned several times in both the Old Testament and New Testament. In Micah 6:5, in the midst of reminding the Israelites of the things he's done for them, God mentions when he directed Balaam to bless them instead of cursing them. Nehemiah also references this same incident in Nehemiah 13 as he's speaking to God's people. Peter mentions Balaam and his donkey in 2 Peter 2 when speaking about false teachers.

Kid Insight

Kids likely have an easier time believing a story about a talking donkey than adults do. Even so, a talking donkey is surprising for anyone! The story of Balaam and his donkey can show kids that God has a sense of humor—and he'll go to surprising lengths to get our attention. This passage is a memorable reminder that God wants us to pay attention to *him* in the midst of life's busy, hectic schedules and distractions. Help kids discover that God wants a two-way relationship with them—a friendship in which both parties listen and respond on an ongoing basis.

You'll need:

- ☐ kid-friendly Bible
- ☐ index cards (1 per child)
- ☐ pencils
- ☐ volunteer to play Balaam
- ☐ Bible-times costume for Balaam
- ☐ stuffed donkey
- ☐ pretend or makeshift sword
- ☐ 2 opaque cups per child, plus 3 extra
- ☐ teaspoon
- ☐ ½-cup measuring cup
- ☐ Magic Slush Powder (found at Walmart and Amazon)
- ☐ pitcher of water
- ☐ *Friends With God Bible Lessons Music* CD and music player
- ☐ crepe paper rolls
- ☐ construction paper
- ☐ fine-tipped markers
- ☐ stickers (about 8-10 per child)
- ☐ glue sticks
- ☐ small individually wrapped candies (about 8-10 per child)
- ☐ child-safe scissors

> If you can't find a volunteer to play Balaam, modify your script slightly and play the role yourself. You'll simply need to have kids close their eyes and put on their imaginations while *you* don the Bible-times costume. If you're female, tweak the script and play this as a friend of Balaam's.

Getting Ready

Place about a teaspoon of Magic Slush Powder into an opaque cup. Fill another cup with 4 ounces of water.

───❧ THE LESSON ❧───

Friend-Maker Icebreaker *(10 minutes)*

SURPRISE IDENTITIES

Welcome kids and introduce yourself.

Say: **Today we'll find out that** <u>God surprises us</u>**. Let's begin with a fun game that may be surprising!**

Have kids sit in a circle. Give each child an index card and a pencil. Have kids each secretly write the name of someone they think everyone will know or will have heard of. It might be the pastor, a school principal, the president, or a popular actor or musician. You can help any kids who struggle to come up with a name.

Have each child hand his or her index card to the person on his or her left, facing down so the person doesn't see what the name is. Kids will hold the cards they received up to their foreheads without looking at the names. Ensure all the names are facing out.

Have everyone stand up. Kids can each find a partner and ask one yes-or-no question about the people named on their foreheads. They might ask if the person is a boy, if the person sings, if the person works at the church, and so on. Circulate and whisper any names into kids' ears if they're having trouble reading the names. Also, help kids think of questions to ask, if needed. Let kids play until they've all figured out the names on their foreheads or as time allows. Ask:

💬 **How did you feel trying to figure out your person's name?**

💬 **What clues helped you the most?**

💬 **Explain whether you were surprised at the end and why.**

Say: **Everyone started out not knowing what was going on, but the clues helped you get closer and closer to the name. In our Bible story today, we'll hear about a man named Balaam** (pronounced "BAY-lum") **who didn't know what was going on. And it wasn't a** *person* **who helped him discover something surprising! We'll find out that** <u>God surprises us</u> **today, too!**

MEET BALAAM

Place the stuffed donkey where "Balaam" can reach it. Balaam should enter and begin a dialogue with kids. You may be needed to assist Balaam with props or lighting. Join in the fun and surprise of talking with this friend of God!

(Enter and begin enthusiastically.)

Hey, friends! I thought this was "bring your pet to church" day, so I brought my donkey. *(Hold up the stuffed donkey.)* **My name's Balaam...and I love my donkey. We've been together for years.** *(Give the donkey a hug.)* **Sure, she can be stubborn sometimes; all donkeys are like that.** *(Hold out the donkey and look at it.)* **Aren't you, donkey?** *Ask:*

💬 **Tell me about a stubborn pet or animal you've met.** *(Take several kids' answers.)*

Sometimes animals can be really stubborn. *(Hold out the donkey.)* **But there was one day my furry friend here was especially headstrong.**

First, you should know that I'm a prophet. That means I give people special messages from God. I'd been traveling down the road to take a message to the king of Moab. When donkeys travel on a rocky road, their hoofs make a noise like this. *(Lead kids in clicking their tongues.)* **You SOUND like donkeys, but I love donkeys so much...I think you should LOOK like them, too!** *(Lead kids in getting on all fours, clicking their tongues as you guide them in a line down a pretend road.)* **We walked and walked—it was a long way.**

Well, I didn't know it, but God wanted to stop me from going down that road! So he sent an angel with a fiery sword to block my path! *(Have the leader jump into the path of the "donkeys," holding up the pretend sword.)*

I guess I'd been daydreaming or thinking about lunch or just not really paying attention, so I didn't see the angel. But my donkey did, and he bolted off the road into the weeds! Quick—pick a side of the road and run there, then stop! *(Have "donkeys" bolt from the path, then stop off the path.)* *Ask:*

💬 **Have you ever been on a trip that didn't turn out the way you thought? What happened?** *(Take a few kids' answers and then move on.)*

I was mad that my donkey took me into the weeds, so I hit her with my stick and got her back on the road. *(Guide the donkeys back onto the road, and lead them in clicking their tongues as they follow you.)* **So we were walking once again.**

(The leader will again jump into the path with the sword.) **And the angel appeared again, but still I didn't see it. This time my donkey tried to squeeze around the angel and crushed my foot against the wall.** *(Have kids act like the donkey, squeezing past the angel and pressing against you. Grab your foot and hop.)* **Ooo, ouch, ouch, ouch!**

That made me pretty mad! So I hit my donkey with a stick again. *(Pretend to reprimand the stuffed donkey.)* **Then we continued on.** *(Lead kids in getting back into a line, clicking their tongues, and walking like donkeys.)*

(The leader will jump into the path with the sword a third time.) **The angel showed up one more time, and my donkey dropped to the ground.** *(Have kids plop flat on the ground.)* **But I was still on her back! I got so mad!** *(Hop up and down as if you're throwing a tantrum.)*

Then I got the surprise of my life: My DONKEY started talking to me! *Ask:*

💬 **Would you believe it if an animal started talking to you? Why or why not?** *(Take a few kids' answers and then move on.)*

I know it's hard to believe—it surprised me, too! But my donkey really did talk. It asked, *(use a different voice for the donkey)* **"Why do you keep hitting me?"**

And I shouted back at my donkey *(hold out your donkey, looking at it, and shout)*, **"You're making me look like a fool! You've never done anything like this before!"**

(Use a different voice for the donkey.) **"Exactly,"** said my donkey. *(Widen your eyes to show surprise and turn the donkey to face kids.)* **Do you believe this?** *(Pause.)*

Just then God opened my eyes, and I saw the angel standing in our way, holding a sword. *(The leader will walk right up next to you with the sword.)*

(Fall to the ground and stay down.) **I dropped to the ground and apologized. Then the angel asked:**

(The leader will point to all the kids and say, "Why are you beating your donkey? I've come to block your way because you're resisting God. Three times your donkey saw me and shied away.") Ask:

💬 **Hmmm. I felt kind of bad when the angel scolded me like that. Has anything like that ever happened to you? Tell about the last time someone called you out for doing something wrong. What was that like?** *(Have kids share in trios for a couple of minutes, then draw attention back to yourself.)*

I tell you, I was surprised. "I'm sorry," I said. "I'll turn around right now." *(Turn to go.)*

(The leader will say, "You can go, but when you meet the king, say only what God tells you to say.")

That means I couldn't just tell the king what he WANTED to hear. So I went on my way. *(Walk around the outside of the group of kids, and then hold out your donkey and shake your head. The leader will stay in place.)* **But I sure never looked at my donkey the same way again!**

(Look at the angel.) **I think I'd better keep going!**

(Wave goodbye and exit.)

Don't Move!

Say: **Since we're learning that** <u>God surprises us</u>**, I have something surprising for you.** Hold up the cup of water. **This is ordinary water.** Let kids pass it around. Have one child take a drink to confirm that it's water.

Pour the water back and forth from the two cups *without* the Magic Slush Powder.

Say: **There's nothing really surprising about that, but what if we add a third cup?** Pour the water into the third cup that contains the Magic Slush Powder. It will instantly turn into slush. Try to pour out the slush and keep tilting the cup until it's upside down. Ask:

💬 **What do you think happened?**

Explain that you used Magic Slush Powder that instantly changed the water into slush. Give each child a cup with a teaspoon of the powder and a cup with 4 ounces of water. Allow time for kids to try the experiment. Play "All Creatures of Our God and King" from the *Friends With God Bible Lessons Music* CD as kids experiment, if you'd like. Ask:

💬 **What surprised you about this experiment?**

Say: **This was a surprising experiment! It reminds me of how Balaam kept moving until God stopped him in a really unexpected way.** <u>God surprises us</u>**! Sometimes God surprises us with his love and forgiveness. Or he surprises us with a beautiful sunrise or a new friend. And sometimes God even surprises us when he says "no" to something we're asking for.**

Listen to this. Read Isaiah 55:9. Ask:

💬 **What does this tell you about God?**

💬 **Why can you trust God's surprises to be for our best even if we don't understand them?**

Say: **God loves us so much—that's why we can trust his surprises!**

SURPRISE GIFT BALLS

Say: **Balaam needed to hear an important message from God, and God did something really surprising to get his attention! Let's make some surprise gifts for people we want to tell about God.**

Show kids how to make a surprise gift ball by wrapping a strip of crepe paper around a piece of candy a few times and then gluing the end of the paper down. Stick a sticker to the outside of the wrapped candy, and wrap *that* little package in another long strip of crepe paper to make a ball. Write "God loves you!" on a small strip of construction paper, and then wrap that into the ball. Explain to kids that they'll wrap a bunch of surprise messages about God, stickers, and candies into the surprise gift ball.

Set out the crepe paper, construction paper, fine-tipped markers, stickers, glue sticks, individually wrapped candies, and child-safe scissors. Help kids make their surprise gift balls. Make sure kids get equal amounts of stickers and candy. Lead kids in brainstorming messages about God to add into their gift balls, such as "God says you're important" and "God made you!" Older kids might have favorite verses they want to add. Every time kids add a gift, they'll cover it with a few layers of crepe paper, wrapping it into a softball-size ball.

Encourage kids to give their gift balls to people they want to tell about God. Say: **God used a donkey to get Balaam's attention, and <u>God surprises us</u> today, too. That's because God is so amazing! Maybe your friend who unwraps your gift ball will be surprised by a special message from God, too.** Lead kids to pray for the people who will be receiving the surprise gift balls.

SURPRISING MESSAGES

Form a circle and have kids sit down.

Say: **God loves each of you so much—he's the best friend we could ever have! That's why we can expect surprises from him. We can't predict all the things God will do or where he'll direct us to go. Let's find out if God has any surprise messages for us now.**

Lead kids in about two minutes of silent prayer. Encourage each child to ask God for a kind message to give to the person to the left of him or her. If kids know the person well, they might share something special that comes to mind. If they don't know the person very well, they might share an important message such as "God says you're important," "God loves and cares for you," or "God made you for a special purpose."

After the moment of prayer, have kids share their special messages with the people to the left of them. Ask:

💬 **Explain whether you were surprised by the special message you received.**

Next, invite kids to talk to God silently about the special message they received and ask God if he has any other special messages for them. Allow a couple of minutes. Ask:

💬 **If you want to, share any special messages you heard from God.**

Say: **It's okay if we didn't all hear a special message from God today. But we can all be sure that God loves us and wants us to be good friends with him. And we can expect God to surprise us in the future with special messages—it might be as we listen to a song or a Bible message or when we're talking to a friend. <u>God surprises us</u>, and we can trust that his surprises are for our best!**

OUR BLOOD RUNS BOLD

BIBLE STORY: **Joshua and the fall of Jericho.** *(Joshua 6)*

BIBLE POINT: <u>**Trusting in God gives us courage.**</u>

BIBLE VERSE: **"This is my command—be strong and courageous! Do not be afraid or discouraged. For the Lord your God is with you wherever you go"** *(Joshua 1:9).*

Bible Insight

▸ Joshua's name means "God is salvation." The Hebrew name for Jesus, *Yeshua*, is a variant of Joshua and has the same meaning.

▸ Born in Egypt, Joshua became Moses' assistant, even accompanying him part of the way up to Mount Sinai to receive the Ten Commandments (Exodus 24:13). God handpicked Joshua to be Moses' successor (Deuteronomy 31:14–15, 23) and equipped him with courage, telling him repeatedly to "be strong and courageous" (Deuteronomy 31:7, 23; Joshua 1:6, 7, 9, 18). Ultimately, Joshua conquered six nations and 31 kings as he led the Israelites to take their promised land.

▸ Jericho was one of the first fortified cities in the region of Canaan. Archaeologists believe there might have been two walls surrounding Jericho—an upper city wall and a lower city wall, with an earthen embankment between. The upper wall may have been as tall as 26 feet and as wide as 6 feet. The lower city wall would've been about 12 to 15 feet tall.

▸ Archaeologists have discovered a section of Jericho's lower wall that remained intact when the rest of the wall fell. Between the upper wall and lower wall, archaeologists discovered houses, some of which had windows that looked out of the city through the lower wall. This portion of the wall faced the hills where the spies could easily run and hide from the pursuing soldiers.

Kid Insight

Kids today face all kinds of situations they aren't quite sure how to handle, from a bully on the playground to a subject in school they don't really understand to their parents' divorce. Our world tells kids to dig deep within themselves and find what they need to make it through. We can be thankful that God doesn't ask us to come up with the solutions to our problems on our own. He's right there to help us. He *wants* to help us. And he has the power to do what we could never do alone. When they're friends with God, kids don't have to face anything alone. God is always right beside them. And when they follow God's directions, the battle's as good as won!

You'll need:

- ☐ kid-friendly Bible
- ☐ volunteer to play Joshua
- ☐ Bible-times costume for Joshua
- ☐ chair
- ☐ bedsheet
- ☐ non-interlocking blocks (handful for each child)
- ☐ "horn" of some kind (this could be a rolled-up piece of paper)
- ☐ disposable plastic cups (1 per child)
- ☐ spoons (1 per child)
- ☐ wax paper
- ☐ cornstarch (about 2 teaspoons per child)
- ☐ white glue (about 1 teaspoon per child)
- ☐ fine-tipped markers
- ☐ toothpicks (1 per child)
- ☐ snack-size resealable plastic bags (1 per child)
- ☐ playground balls (1 for every 4 or 5 kids)
- ☐ painter's tape
- ☐ teaspoon
- ☐ *Friends With God Bible Lessons Music* CD and music player

If you can't find a volunteer to play Joshua, modify your script slightly and play the role yourself. You'll simply need to have kids close their eyes and put on their imaginations while *you* don the Bible-times costume. If you're female and would prefer not to play a male character, tweak the script and play this as a bystander.

Getting Ready

Make a sample clay disk for your example.

⸙ THE LESSON ⸙

Friend-Maker Icebreaker *(10 minutes)*

KNOCK DOWN THE WALL

Welcome kids and introduce yourself.

Say: **There are things we expect to just work. A chair will hold us up when we sit on it. A car will start when we turn the key. A wall will stand strong and hold up the ceiling. But sometimes things don't work right and we have to figure out why.** Ask:

💬 **Tell a friend about a time you had something that wasn't working and you had to figure out why.**
Give kids a chance to share with a friend.

Say: **Walls are usually pretty sturdy things. We don't worry about them falling down on us. Let's play a game where we need to figure out what, or who, is making our wall fall down.**

Have kids sit down in a circle. Choose one willing child to be the Detective, and have that child sit in the center of the circle. Ask the Detective to sit with eyes closed while you choose someone to be the Wall-breaker. Make sure everyone in the circle knows who the Wall-breaker is. Once the Wall-breaker has been chosen, the Detective can begin watching.

Say: **We're going to pretend our circle is a wall. Somewhere in our circle is a one-person wrecking crew, ready to tear down our wall brick by brick. If the Wall-breaker winks at you, you'll lie down as your part of the wall falls down. It's our Detective's job to catch the Wall-breaker before the entire wall falls down. The Detective will get only three guesses, so the Detective will need to watch carefully. As for our wall, we don't want to help the Detective, so don't watch the Wall-breaker too closely.** (If the Wall-breaker doesn't know how to wink, have him or her use a long blink instead.)

The Detective will watch and try to determine who the Wall-breaker is. If the Detective guesses correctly or the entire wall falls down, the game begins again with a new Detective and a new Wall-breaker.

Play "I Will Not Be Afraid" from the *Friends With God Bible Lessons Music* CD while kids play.

Say: **Walls don't usually fall down that easily. But we're going to hear about someone today who faced an enormous wall and an even bigger challenge. This friend discovered that** <u>Trusting in God gives us courage</u>**. With God's help, we can face great obstacles.**

Bible Adventure *(20 minutes)*

MEET JOSHUA

Have a chair handy for "Joshua" to use. Place the bedsheet, blocks, and "horn" where Joshua can reach them. Joshua should enter and begin a dialogue with kids. You will be needed to assist Joshua with props, including using the bedsheet to knock down the wall. Join in the fun and surprise of talking with this friend of God!

(Enter and plop down in the chair.)

Phew! What a day! *(Pretend to brush dust off your clothes.)* **Thanks for inviting me to visit. Sorry I'm so worn out...and dirty! I'm Joshua, the leader of God's chosen people. And after YEARS of waiting, we've FINALLY begun to take the land God promised us hundreds of years ago.** *Ask:*

💬 **Have you ever had to wait a REALLY long time for something? Tell me about that.** *(Give kids a chance to respond.)*

Well, let me back up and tell you how all this happened. God rescued us from slavery in Egypt a little more than 40 years ago. Moses, our leader, sent me, my friend Caleb, and 10 other men as spies to check out the land God had promised. I'll never forget THAT adventure! *(Move around the room, hiding behind furniture or even kids, acting like a spy. Hold your hands up to your eyes like binoculars.)* **The land was amazing, but it was full of strong, powerful people. Most of my people, the Israelites, didn't have the courage to go into the land. All they could see were the mighty people we would have to fight. They didn't trust God. Caleb and I tried to convince them that God was bigger than their fears, but they just wouldn't listen. So we had to wait 40 MORE YEARS.** *Ask:*

💬 **Have YOU ever let fear keep you from doing something you really wanted to do? Tell a friend about that.** *(Give kids a minute to share with a friend, then draw attention back to yourself.)*

Now, 40 years later, Moses is gone. God told ME to be strong and courageous and to lead the Israelites into the land. This time, the people obeyed. But when we crossed into the land, the first thing we saw was Jericho—a huge city surrounded by the biggest wall I've ever seen. The wall was so big that they could drive a chariot on top of it! Wait, I need some help so you can understand just how incredible this was! *(Have kids stand up and link arms in a circle to form their own wall.)*

One night, I sneaked out of camp to check out the city. *(Sneak around the "wall," and try to gently pry your way into the circle while the kids work to keep you out.)* **I stood at the bottom of the giant wall and craned my neck to see the top.** *(Crane your neck like you're looking up really high.)* **Yep, by all accounts, we didn't have a chance. Defeating Jericho seemed impossible.** *(Have kids sit back down.)* *Ask:*

💬 **Think about something in YOUR life that seems impossible.** *(Give kids about 30 seconds to think.)*

Maybe YOU can imagine how we felt.

Then I looked up and saw a man standing in front of me with a sword. *(Jump back as if startled.)* **I asked him, "Are you on our side or the side of our enemy?"**

"Neither," he said. "I am the commander of GOD'S army."

I asked him what God wanted us to do, and he gave me the STRANGEST instructions. But he promised that GOD had given us the city. Well, Jericho still looked pretty scary, but I knew that if God had promised us the city, it was as good as ours. In spite of the odds, GOD gave me courage.

The people of Jericho had locked the gates tight so no one could go in or out. THEY were

afraid of US. Well, ACTUALLY, they were afraid of our God. They knew what I knew: God can do anything! So while the king of Jericho and his people hid behind their mighty wall, my people and I simply followed God's instructions, even though what God told us to do seemed really strange. *Ask:*

💬 **Has an adult ever asked you to do something you didn't understand, like stay away from a certain place or not eat certain foods? Find a friend and tell about that and why you think the adult gave you that instruction.** *(Have kids turn to a partner and share their answers while you lay out the bedsheet in the center of the room. Give kids the blocks, and encourage them to stack them into a wall on the sheet, leaving enough room to walk around it.)*

So here's what God told us to do: We were supposed to silently march around the city once a day for six days. This was a bit scary. I mean, what if the soldiers from Jericho ran out and attacked us? We had no BATTLE plan. This made some of our soldiers pretty nervous. But we knew God had a plan, so we trusted him and had courage. Why don't you walk around your wall like we did? *(Lead kids in walking silently around their block wall.)*

On the seventh day, our instructions were a bit different. Everyone marched around the city SEVEN times. When we stopped, our priests blew their horns, and then everyone shouted as loud as they could. Why don't we give that a try? I'll blow this horn, and all of you need to shout as loud as you can. Are you ready? *(Blow the "horn" and give kids a chance to shout at the wall.)*

The great walls of Jericho shook, cracked, and thundered to the ground! *(Let kids help you give the bedsheet a sharp tug so the wall falls down.)*

Our enemy was defeated, and we hadn't even had to fight. GOD fought for us. And now the great city of Jericho was nothing but a pile of rubble.

As for my people and me, we didn't win the battle with stronger men or sharper swords. We won because we had the courage to trust in God and obey him. It wasn't that we weren't scared. Having courage doesn't mean you aren't scared. But you can trust that God is bigger than anything you're afraid of.

Well, I'm pretty exhausted. It's been a LONG day! I think I'll head back to my tent.

(Wave goodbye and exit.)

POCKET COURAGE

Say: **When we're facing a big challenge, like Joshua did, it can be easy to forget that God is with us. Sometimes we need something to remind us that** <u>trusting in God gives us courage</u>**. Let's make something to help us remember to trust God because he never leaves us.**

Give each child a disposable cup, a spoon, and a small piece of wax paper. Let each child measure two spoonfuls of cornstarch into his or her cup. Then help kids each mix in 1 spoonful of white glue and stir until the mixture reaches a claylike consistency. (If the mixture is too sticky, add more cornstarch. If it's too crumbly, add more glue.) Have kids knead the clay with their hands until they can roll it into a small ball.

Have each child place his or her ball onto the wax paper and gently smash it down until it's about 1 to 1½ inches in diameter. Give each child a toothpick and some markers. Have kids use the toothpicks to carefully scratch (or make from a series of small holes) the words "Trust God" in the clay. They can decorate around the words as well, if they'd like. Show them how to carefully use the markers to add color to their designs. Let the clay sit for a minute or so to let that side dry a little.

While kids are waiting, say: **Joshua and the Israelites could never have conquered Jericho on their own. They needed God to fight the battle for them.** Ask:

💬 **What challenge in your life do you need God's help with?**

Help kids get started by sharing something you need God's help with in your own life. Then have kids share their own thoughts with a partner.

Next, guide kids in carefully flipping their clay disks to the other side and using the toothpicks and markers to write "Have Courage" on that side and add any decorations. Let the clay sit out as long as possible before placing it in the resealable plastic bags for kids to take home. Instruct kids to set their clay out in the open air to finish drying when they get home.

Say: **God promised Joshua he would always be with him. Listen to this.** Read Joshua 1:9 aloud.

Say: **God promises he'll be with us, too.** <u>Trusting God gives us courage</u>**, just like it did for Joshua. Once your clay disk is completely dry, keep it in your pocket or somewhere it can remind *you* to trust God and have courage.**

Knock Down the Wall

Say: **In Bible times, lots of cities had big, thick walls to protect the people inside. The people of Jericho might have trusted in their walls, but God is stronger than bricks and mud! Let's play a game that will remind us of the walls of Jericho.**

Form teams of four or five kids, and give each team a ball. Direct each team to pick a spot along one wall, and have each child bring a handful of blocks to the team's designated spot. (It's okay if each team has a different number of blocks.) Give teams one minute to stack all their blocks into a wall. Make sure the structures aren't flat against the classroom wall. Use painter's tape to mark a line on the opposite side of the room. Have one member of the team stay by the block wall and the others line up behind the tape line.

Say: **Each member of your team will take a turn rolling a ball, bowling style, down to the other end, trying to knock down your wall. The teammate down by the wall is the "Spy" who'll grab the ball and roll it back to the next person in your line. When no blocks are still standing on top of one another, your team must race to your wall and rebuild it. Then a new person can stay behind as the Spy and you can start again.**

Allow kids to continue playing as long as time allows, and then gather them back together.

Say: **The people in Jericho had a strong, thick wall to protect them. But the Bible says they were *still* afraid of God's people! They'd heard all that God had done for the Israelites. When the Israelites trusted God, he gave them the courage to conquer that city. <u>Trusting God gives us courage</u>, too!** Ask:

💬 **What things do people today trust to keep them safe?**

💬 **How is God different from those things?**

Say: **When we trust in other things, sometimes they let us down. But if we trust in God, we can know that he *always* keeps his promises. <u>Trusting in God gives *us* courage</u>. God is *bigger* than anything we face.**

STEP OF FAITH

Say: **Joshua trusted God to do something he could never do on his own: conquer Jericho. God commanded Joshua to trust him and promised that he would always be with Joshua.** Read aloud Joshua 1:9.

Say: **Sometimes we face things in our own lives that seem too big for us to handle alone. God wants us to trust him, and he'll give us courage. That doesn't mean God will always help us the way we want him to or expect him to. Joshua may have wished Jericho's wall would just fall before they arrived. But when we trust that God loves us and has a plan for us, we can know he's doing what's best, and he's *always* with us.**

Gather kids in a circle, and let each person take a block. Ask kids to think of something that's a big challenge for them, letting them know they won't have to share it aloud. Share your own example, such as finding a new job, finishing a hard project at work, or watching a family member struggle with poor health. Then have kids take turns placing their blocks in the center of the circle to make a thick wall. (If you have a lot of kids, make the wall thicker rather than taller, since kids will have to step over it.) Then have kids form a line on one side of the wall.

Say: **As you step up to this pile of blocks, whisper a prayer. Ask God to help you deal with this challenge, just as he helped his people so long ago. Pray, "God, please give me the courage to..." and tell God what you're struggling with. Then step over the blocks, knowing that you can trust God to give you courage in that situation.**

Start the activity by stepping up to the pile yourself and whispering a prayer. Then step over the block wall. Encourage kids to step up to the pile one at a time, whisper a prayer, and step over the wall. Remind the remaining kids to be respectful as their friends all get a chance to pray.

Close the prayer: **God, thank you that you always hear our prayers and we can trust you to help us, no matter what we may be facing. Thank you that trusting you gives us courage. In Jesus' name, amen.**

Keeping It Together

BIBLE STORY: **Ruth and Naomi help each other.** *(Ruth 1–2)*

BIBLE POINT: <u>**God is our friend.**</u>

BIBLE VERSE: **"So now we can rejoice in our wonderful new relationship with God because our Lord Jesus Christ has made us friends of God"** *(Romans 5:11).*

Bible Insight

▸ In the laws and regulations given to the Israelites, God made provisions for the poor and the foreigners living among them. God commanded harvesters to leave the outer edges of the field untouched so that those who had no field could reap there. He also instructed them *not* to go back and pick up anything dropped during the harvest, so the poor could gather (or "glean") these pieces for themselves. God gave this instruction three times in the books of the Law (Leviticus 19:9-10; 23:22; Deuteronomy 24:19-22). Boaz went above and beyond this regulation in Ruth's case, even instructing his workers to purposely drop grain (Ruth 2:15-16).

▸ Though *God* made special provisions for foreigners living among the Israelites, the Israelites themselves didn't always extend such a welcome. Therefore, the presence of Ruth in Jesus' genealogy is significant. Ruth is one of four women mentioned in Jesus' genealogy, all four of whom are believed to have been Gentiles: Tamar, Rahab, Ruth, and Bathsheba (Matthew 1:2-6). In this way, God reminded Israel, as well as the early church, that he wasn't the God of Israel alone but the God of all nations.

▸ Ruth embraced Naomi's God as her own, and they both trusted in his care as they returned to Bethlehem alone and in need. Ruth showed herself to be a "virtuous" woman by her actions (Ruth 3:11). Ruth's faith in God and inward character mattered most. The same is true for us. God has always been more concerned about the condition of our hearts than anything else, as he reminded Samuel in 1 Samuel 16:7.

▸ Moab wasn't exactly an enemy to Israel, but they weren't friends either. The Moabites treated the Israelites with hostility as God's people traveled through the area on their way to the Promised Land. First, a Moabite king summoned Balaam to curse the Israelites (Numbers 22–24). Then the Moabites lured the Israelites to worship Baal, leading to a plague in the wilderness (Numbers 25:1-5). God told the Israelites, "As long as you live, you must never promote the welfare and prosperity of the Ammonites or Moabites" (Deuteronomy 23:6). Although God rejected Moab as a nation, he still loved its individuals, as we see in the life of Ruth.

Kid Insight

Friendships are critically important for kids. But with changes in classes, schools, and even neighborhoods, friends can often come and go. Many kids don't feel like they have any true friends. Kids need to know that there's one friend who'll always be by their side. Proverbs 18:24 says, "There are 'friends' who destroy each other, but a real friend sticks closer than a brother." Jesus is that friend. Kids need to know that no matter what happens with other friends in their lives, Jesus will *always* be there.

You'll need:

- [ ] kid-friendly Bible
- [ ] volunteer to play Naomi
- [ ] Bible-times costume for Naomi
- [ ] doll wrapped in a blanket
- [ ] chair (ideally a rocking chair)
- [ ] large basket filled with shredded paper
- [ ] 3 hula hoops
- [ ] various colors of 9x12 construction paper (1 sheet will serve 2 kids, but you'll need a few extras)
- [ ] child-safe scissors
- [ ] tape
- [ ] 3x5 cards (1 per child)
- [ ] pens or pencils (1 per child)
- [ ] *Friends With God Bible Lessons Music* CD and music player

If you can't find a volunteer to play Naomi, modify your script slightly and play the role yourself. You'll simply need to have kids close their eyes and put on their imaginations while *you* don the Bible-times costume. If you're male, tweak the script and play this as Boaz.

Getting Ready

Cut construction paper into 3x9-inch strips, making two strips per child. You'll also need one 2x9-inch paper strip per child.

···❧ THE LESSON ❧···

Friend-Maker Icebreaker *(10 minutes)*

DIFFERENT AND ALIKE

Welcome kids and introduce yourself.

Say: **God has made us all wonderfully unique. Many of us love vanilla ice cream. Many of us like cats. Many of us enjoy riding our bikes. But not everyone loves all three of those things. Each of us is a completely unique combination of likes and dislikes.**

Let's see what ways we're like our friends and what ways we're different. I'm going to ask a question, and you'll call out your answer and then gather with everyone who's answering the same way. We'll start with an easy one. Ask:

💬 **What's your favorite ice cream flavor?**

Encourage kids to call out their favorite flavor of ice cream and move around the room until they find those who have the same answer. It's okay if a child is the only one with a certain like or dislike. When most kids have gathered into groups, have each group call out its answer. Repeat the process with the following questions, or feel free to come up with some of your own.

💬 **What's your favorite pizza topping?**

💬 **What's your favorite thing to do in your free time?**

💬 **What's your favorite type of pet?**

💬 **What's your favorite sport (to play or watch)?**

💬 **What's your favorite color?**

💬 **Where's your favorite place to go on vacation?**

Say: **You probably met up with the same people a few times in our game, but I doubt any two of you were in the same group every time. We're all different. But those differences can make being friends even more fun.** Ask:

💬 **Think about a good friend. In what ways is that person like you?**

💬 **In what ways is that person different?**

Give kids a minute or two to share with those around them.

Say: **When we have friends who are different from us, we can learn to appreciate those things about them. Who knows? We may even find that we learn to like something new! Today we're going to meet two women who were very different, but they became the best of friends.**

MEET NAOMI

Place the rocking chair and doll where "Naomi" can reach them. Set the basket filled with shredded paper nearby. Naomi should enter and begin a dialogue with kids. You will be needed to assist Naomi with the basket. Join in the fun and surprise of talking with this friend of God!

Friendly Tip: If you have the ability to move from one space to another, let kids experience "moving" with you and your family. Lay the doll in a "bed," then lead kids to another space or on a trip around your church building. Then lead them back after they discuss what they'd miss the most if *they* had to move.

(Enter cradling the doll and shushing as if you're trying to soothe a baby. Sit down in the chair. If it's a rocking chair, rock back and forth as you talk.)

Hello, friends. My name's Naomi. I was just about to tell my new baby grandson, Obed, a bedtime story. It's actually MY story of how God taught me what it means to be a good friend.

Many years ago, things were hard here in Israel. No rain fell, and no food would grow. My husband and I, along with our two boys, were about to starve! *Ask:*

💬 Have you ever been really hungry? I mean REALLY hungry? Tell a friend about it. *(Let kids share with a few friends for about a minute, and then continue.)*

We moved to a country called Moab that had plenty of food. Things went well at first, but then my husband died. We were so sad.

But in time, my sons got married to two lovely women named Ruth and Orpah...and things seemed to be getting better. I still missed my home in Bethlehem, but we started making a new home. *(Smile.)* I really liked my new daughters-in-law, especially Ruth. When she married my son, we became relatives, but then something special happened: We also became FRIENDS. And like lots of friends do, when hard times came, we helped each other. *(Sigh.)* Well, MORE sad times were in store...because both my sons died. Ruth lost her husband, and I'd lost both my sons. We needed to comfort each other. *Ask:*

💬 When has a friend helped YOU through a hard time? *(Let a few kids share with the group, and then continue.)*

Ruth and Orpah were the only family I had left. With no husbands to support us, things were going to get REALLY hard for all of us. I told the young women to go back home to their own mothers so they could marry again. As for me, I felt sad to say goodbye, but I knew I needed to be with the rest of my family in Bethlehem.

But Ruth said "No!" She wouldn't abandon me. I told her that moving to Bethlehem meant she would leave behind EVERYTHING she knew. *Ask:*

💬 If you had to leave behind everything in your life, what would you miss the most?

Ruth promised to stick with me. She told me something I'll never forget *(look up as if remembering)*: "Wherever you go, I will go; wherever you live, I will live. Your people will be my people, and your God will be my God."

(Touch your hand to your heart.) That meant so much to me! So we started our journey TOGETHER. Traveling to Bethlehem was hard! I hadn't been there in a long time...and what if we couldn't even find food? I felt a little nervous about all that. *Ask:*

💬 Where is a place YOU'RE nervous about going to?

I tried to tell Ruth what Bethlehem would be like and who we would meet there. I told her about our God. I remembered that people called him a friend to the helpless. That SURE felt like us. When we got to my hometown of Bethlehem, friends and family welcomed us with open arms. Ruth, faithful friend that she is, went straight to work gathering grain in the fields. She wanted to do her part to help us both have something to eat and live a good life. I realized that God had given me a friend who would stand by me. Maybe he hadn't forgotten me after all.

(Have the leader spread the shredded paper on the floor around the room.)

It wasn't easy for Ruth. Farming is hard work. She went to a nearby barley field and picked up the extra grain the harvesters left behind. *(Motion to the shredded paper.)* Would you pick up the extra "grain" our harvester left behind? Let's see how quickly you can gather the grain and put it back in the basket.

(Give kids a minute to gather up all the shredded paper and return it to the basket.)

That may not have seemed hard, but imagine doing it not just for a couple of minutes but out in the hot sun ALL DAY. Every day. Over and over and over! *(Lay the back of your hand across your forehead as if hot.)* Whew! Just thinking about it makes me tired!

But that's what Ruth did so she and I would have something to eat. Soon Boaz, the owner of the field, noticed her working. He'd heard about what a true friend she'd been to me and how she'd left her own family to help me.

Boaz gave her food and water. He watched out for her and let her gather grain as long as she wanted. When she showed me all the food she had collected, I was so excited! *(Hop out of the chair excitedly. Then remember the baby, if you're still holding him, and carefully sit back down.)* I was so thankful she had chosen to be such a good friend. I definitely couldn't have done that on my own.

Ruth later married Boaz, and they had little baby…Obed! *(Proudly show the doll to the kids.)* Ruth had kept her promise to go where I went, to let my people become her people, and to have faith in my God. Ruth and I aren't just friends with each other; we're friends with God, too. Ruth's friendship reminded me that <u>God's always my friend</u>, and he's the best friend anyone could EVER hope for. He hadn't abandoned me; he was with me all the time. Maybe YOU'VE experienced God's friendship. *Ask:*

💬 What's one way being friends with a person is like being friends with God?

Even when we feel like we don't have a great friend here on earth to help us, God never leaves us. <u>God is always our very best friend</u>.

Well, I'd better put this little guy to bed. Thanks for letting me come and chat with you!

(Exit.)

TEAM TAG

Say: **Ruth and Naomi had to work together just to survive as they traveled and started a new life in Bethlehem. Sometimes working with our friends is easy, and sometimes it's a little bit harder.**

Let's play a game and practice our teamwork.

Choose three willing kids to be "Taggers," and give each a hula hoop. Have everyone, including the Taggers, spread out around the room.

Say: **This game is just like regular tag, except that the Taggers hold hula hoops around their waists as they run. When you're tagged, *you* hop inside the hula hoop and help tag someone else. When you do, that person will join you inside the hula hoop, too. Your tagging team can tag only one person at a time. Are you ready? Go!**

Play "Your Friend" from the *Friends With God Bible Lessons Music* CD while kids enjoy the game. Allow kids to play until everyone has been tagged except three kids, or until all the hula hoops are too full to add any more kids. Then have the kids left untagged take the hula hoops and become the new Taggers. Continue playing as time allows.

When you've finished playing, gather kids back together and collect the hula hoops. Ask:

- 💬 **Was it easier or harder to tag people as a group? Why?**
- 💬 **When is it hard to get along or work together with your friends?**
- 💬 **What helps you work better with your friends?**

Say: **Sometimes we need to be willing to compromise and not do things our own way when we're playing with friends. We can't always do things our own way with God, either. <u>God is our friend</u>. But unlike our friends here on earth, God always knows what's best.** Ask:

- 💬 **When might God's way be different from your way?**

Share your own example, such as reaching out in friendship to someone outside your circle of friends. Then encourage kids to share with those around them.

Say: **God loves us, so we can always trust that his ways are the best ways. Even though Naomi's life didn't go the way she would've planned it, God was her friend through it all. And he had an even better plan! Ruth and Boaz's son, Obed, was King David's grandpa and part of Jesus' family tree. Pretty awesome, huh?**

Woven Together

Say: **Ruth and Naomi are great examples of what it means to be good friends. As we spend time with a friend, our hearts become woven together like Ruth and Naomi's were. Let's make something to remind us what it's like to be true friends.**

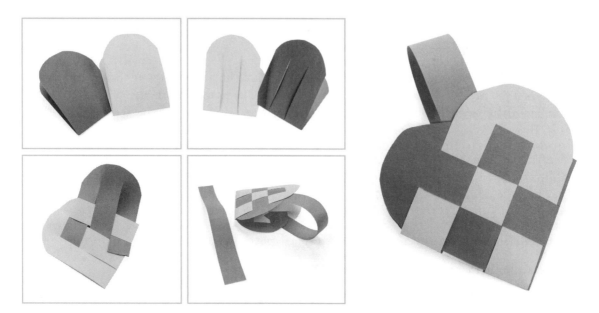

Give each child two construction paper strips of different colors and a pair of scissors. Show kids how to fold each strip in half and cut the ends so they're rounded. Then have kids cut two equally spaced slits into the folded ends of the paper to create three loops. Slits should be long enough to accommodate the whole width of the other strip.

Have kids hold one piece in each hand. Show kids how to weave the loops of the two pieces together by taking the bottom loop of the paper in their right hand and feeding it through the first loop of the paper in their left hand. Then slide it over (and around) the second loop, *not on top of it*. Then feed it through the last loop again, just like you did on the first one.

Then have kids take the next loop of the paper in their right hand and slide it over the first loop, through the second loop, and over the third loop. Guide kids in repeating this process for the remaining loop of the paper in their right hand. Keep tape handy in case kids rip their loops.

Give each child a 2-inch paper strip to tape to the inside of both sides of the heart to create a handle for the basket.

Say: **When we grow closer to a friend, our hearts become connected, like the hearts in our craft.** Ask:

💬 **What are some ways we can grow closer to our friends?**

💬 **Which of those things can help us grow closer to God, too?**

Say: **When we spend time with God, talk to him, and listen to him, our hearts grow more and more connected with his heart, too. <u>God is our friend</u>, and he's the very best friend of all.**

THE PRAYER OF A FRIEND

Have kids get into groups of four or five.

Say: <u>God is our friend</u>, **and we can talk to him anytime about anything. We call talking to God** *praying*. **One of the greatest things we can do for our friends here on earth is pray for them. We can pray for our friends right now. Let's start by finding out what our friends need.**

Give each child a 3x5 card and a pen or pencil. Encourage kids to write down prayer requests to share with their group. A request could be a friend they want to know Jesus, a physical need, or just that God would be with them. (Make sure kids don't use names if the request is sensitive in nature.) If kids don't have a specific request, their friends can simply pray that they would know God better and become closer friends with him.

Say: **Not only can we talk to our friend God about our own needs, but we can also talk to him about our friends' needs.** Encourage kids to trade cards so each child can pray for one other member of the group.

Say: **Now let's talk to our very best friend, God, about the needs of our friends here.** Encourage kids to pray for one another, either silently or out loud.

After a few minutes, close the prayer: **God, we thank you that you're our very best friend and you love it when we talk with you. Thank you that you always hear our prayers. In Jesus' name, amen.**

Encourage kids to take their friends' prayer requests home and continue to pray.

A Prayer and A Promise

BIBLE STORY: **God hears Hannah's prayer.** *(1 Samuel 1:9-28)*

BIBLE POINT: **God hears us.**

BIBLE VERSE: **"And we are confident that he hears us whenever we ask for anything that pleases him"** *(1 John 5:14).*

Bible Insight

▸ Many times, we talk about how Hannah couldn't have a child...and then God hears her prayers and she has Samuel. God answered Hannah's prayers! But oftentimes we don't acknowledge that God gave Hannah *more* than just one child. God answered Hannah's prayers by giving her far more than what she asked for—Samuel *and* three other sons and two daughters!

▸ Let's not forget that Hannah wasn't the only one asking God for a child. The priest, Eli, prayed for God to give Hannah a son, too. God hears our prayers when we cry out to him for something we desperately need or desire, *and* he hears our prayers and answers them when we pray on the behalf of others. Plus, the Bible says Eli didn't stop praying for Hannah after God answered their prayers; he continued to pray for God's blessings over Hannah as time went on.

▸ The Bible includes other accounts of women who cried out to God for children. God blessed Sarah with a child when she was about 90 or 91 years old (Genesis 17; 21). God answered Isaac's prayers for his wife after a period of infertility by giving her twins (Genesis 25). Jacob's wife, Rachel, was also infertile, and after her prayers, God eventually gave her baby Joseph (Genesis 30).

Kid Insight

Because we can't see God with our eyes or touch him with our hands the way we do a human, kids may not think to go to God when they're in distress. They might cry to a parent or other relative, although parents aren't always able to do anything to "fix" the child's problem. Hannah's example of crying bitterly to God shows kids that they can cry out to God, too. God wants them to share their fears, worries, and sadness with him. And God is more powerful than anyone! What a comfort to discover that such a mighty, awesome God bends down to listen (Psalm 116:2) and tenderly cares.

You'll need:

- ☐ kid-friendly Bible
- ☐ volunteer to play Hannah
- ☐ Bible-times costume for Hannah
- ☐ spray bottle filled with water
- ☐ chairs (1 per child)
- ☐ gallon-size resealable plastic bags (2 per child)
- ☐ paper
- ☐ pens
- ☐ various items for care kits, such as bandages, deodorant, snack bars, combs, toothbrushes, and toothpaste
- ☐ *Friends With God Bible Lessons Music* CD and music player

> If you can't find a volunteer to play Hannah, modify your script slightly and play the role yourself. You'll simply need to have kids close their eyes and put on their imaginations while *you* don the Bible-times costume. If you're male, tweak the script and play this as Samuel.

Getting Ready

Contact a local shelter or outreach organization, and find out what items they need for homeless people in your community. Be aware of any things that are *not* acceptable so you can be assured that the care kits kids make will be helpful and usable.

·❦·THE LESSON❦·

Friend-Maker Icebreaker *(10 minutes)*

FRIENDSHIP PHONE

Welcome kids and introduce yourself. Ask:

💬 **What's your favorite sound to listen to? Why?**

Share your own favorite sound and tell why, then let kids respond.

Say: **Today we'll discover that *God* likes to listen to *you*! To get started, let's play a listening game.** Have kids line up, and explain that they'll be playing "Friendship Phone." The first person in line will whisper one sentence, explaining one fun thing he or she did this week, into the second person's ear. This sentence will be passed down the line until it gets to the last person, who will share aloud what he or she heard. Then have the first person move to the end of the line, and the person who is now first will share something he or she did this week. Continue until all the kids have shared. Ask:

💬 **What's something you heard that was interesting?**

💬 **Tell about someone you enjoy listening to—maybe a teacher, friend, or family member who tells fun stories. Why do you like listening to that person?**

💬 **Tell about someone who is a good listener when *you* talk.**

Say: **Friends listen to each other. And God is a great listener! <u>God hears us any time we talk to him.</u> Let's find out from a visiting friend how God listened to her.**

MEET HANNAH

Place the spray bottle of water nearby. "Hannah" should enter and begin a dialogue with kids. You may be needed to assist Hannah with props or lighting. Join in the fun and surprise of talking with this friend of God!

(Enter with a serious tone.)

Hi, friends. My name is Hannah, and I'm so glad to be surrounded by friends like you. Friends care about each other's hopes and dreams—things we wish for. For me, there was only one thing I wanted in life: a son. But year after year went by, and nothing. *Ask:*

💬 What's something YOU wanted more than anything else? *(Let kids share in pairs for about a minute, then take a few responses from the group.)*

Let's see who had to wait the longest. If you had to wait a day to get the thing you wanted so badly, raise your hand. *(Pause.)* Keep your hand up if you had to wait a week. *(Pause, and then continue asking about longer periods of time until you see who waited the longest...or is still waiting.)*

Well, I waited years and years, hoping to have a baby. And year after year, *(sadly)* no child. Was it never going to happen? *(Points to kids.)* Have YOU ever given up on something? Like you wanted your team to win just one basketball game and then you kept losing. Or you wanted your parents to take you to Disneyland, but it just seemed like it would never happen. *(Ask kids to explain if they say they have.)*

I waited so long that I wondered if it was EVER going to happen. Still, I went to the Tabernacle—that's sort of like your church—to beg God to give me a son. I mean, I really begged. *(Invite kids to demonstrate their best begging poses. For example, they might get on one knee or lie facedown on the floor. Point out various poses to the rest of the kids.)*

When I was begging God, I even made a promise. I said that if God would give me a son, I promised to let my son go live with the church leader and be raised to be a church leader. *Ask:*

💬 Let's hear some promises you've made to get something you really wanted.

💬 Did you keep those promises when you got what you wanted? What was that like?

My promise wasn't easy—I couldn't imagine what it might be like to let my son go to live far away from me. Especially after waiting so long to even HAVE a baby! But I was desperate! At the Tabernacle, I cried and prayed out loud. I must have looked strange! Show me your wildest cries. *(Walk among kids and point out the silliest cries you see.)*

Who knows? My tears could've been falling so hard that I might've gotten the people around me wet. *(Have the leader spray kids with the water bottle.)*

One thing I do know: My crying was so loud that Eli, the priest, asked me what was wrong. *Ask:*

💬 Who comforts you when YOU'RE sad? *(Take a few answers.)*

When I told Eli how sad I was, Eli assured me that God would answer my prayer. And he said he'd pray for me, too! Friends do that. *(Have kids pair up and share something they want prayer for. Then have them pray quietly for a moment.)*

Well, God heard my prayers, and he answered them!

I named my beautiful baby boy Samuel. I loved baby Samuel so much! I took care of him just like any good parent would do. Sometimes parents can look a little silly caring for their babies, huh? *(Lead kids in pretending to rock a baby in their arms, comfort a crying baby, or make silly noises at a baby.)* When Samuel was just a few years old, I knew it was time to keep my promise. *(Take a deep breath.)* I took him back to Eli at the Tabernacle.

Even though I missed my little boy, he grew up serving God for the rest of his life. God heard me! *(Sniffle and pretend to wipe a tear.)* Excuse me. Telling you my story has made me just as thankful all over again. I'm going to talk to God and thank him. I know he'll hear me—he always does!

(Wave goodbye and exit.)

LISTEN FOR LEMONS

Say: <u>God hears us</u>, just as he heard Hannah! Let's play a fun listening game to help us think about that.

Have kids form a circle with chairs. Once the circle is arranged, remove one chair and tighten the circle. Have one child stand in the center. Assign each child (including the person in the center) one of the following fruits: apple, banana, lemon, mango, kiwi. (If you have fewer than 10 kids, use only three of the fruits.)

To start, the child in the center will call any of the five fruits, and all the kids who are that fruit will have to get up from their seats and find new seats to sit in. The child in the center will try to grab one of the open seats before anyone else gets it. Whoever is left standing is the new Caller. Kids can call more than one fruit at once or say "fruit salad," which means *everyone* must find a new seat!

As kids play, turn up the volume on the song "God Is Listening" from the *Friends With God Bible Lessons Music* CD so the fruits aren't always easy to hear. Continue for several rounds, as time allows. Ask:

🗩 **What made it hard to hear what was said?**

🗩 **Do you think it's ever hard for God to listen to us? Explain your thoughts on that.**

Say: **Sometimes when we talk to God, we might wonder if he hears us. After all, he has a *lot* of big, important things to pay attention to! We might not hear an audible answer, but <u>God hears us</u>. He wants us to talk to him, and he's always listening. We don't have to worry about him being distracted or missing our prayers because of all the other voices talking to him. He listens carefully to each of us.**

CARE KITS

Have kids form pairs.

Say: **Quickly think of something you might need on a typical day at school.** Pause for 10 seconds while kids think. **Now have the person sitting closest to me silently act out that need while the partner guesses the need.** Pause while kids act out needing things like a pencil, a drink of water, a friend, or a snack. Then have partners switch roles. Ask:

💬 **What was it like to not have a voice to express your need?**

Say: **When you need something, you can ask a friend, a parent, or a teacher. Sometimes God uses people like that to answer our prayers. But there are people in our world who don't have that kind of support around them. They may feel like they don't even have a voice to call out to God...or anyone.**

God might use *you* to answer someone's cry. You can be the hands of God when you serve others! Let's practice that right now. Give each child a gallon-size resealable plastic bag, and set out all the supplies you brought for the care kits.

Lead kids in putting together bags of supplies for local people who are homeless or in need. Have kids write short notes to the people who will receive them, letting them know that God cares about their needs and he hears them when they cry out to him.

As kids work, invite them to talk about needs other people might be praying about that kids could meet to show those people that God hears them. For example, if there's a lonely child at school, they can be a friend to the child. Reinforce the fact that <u>God hears us</u> and wants to take care of our needs like he did for Hannah. He might not always answer in the way we think he will, but he will answer.

Say: **God listened to Hannah in Old Testament times, and Jesus' friends also knew God heard them. God's friend John wrote a letter to new Christians, telling them to be confident that God will hear their prayers. Listen to this.** Read aloud 1 John 5:14. Ask:

💬 **How can this passage encourage you when you pray?**

After your lesson, deliver the care kits to a local shelter.

PRAY FOR THE VOICELESS

Have each child touch the care kit he or she made.

Say: **Let's pray for the people we made these bags for. We might ask God to help the people find jobs or homes. We might pray for them to meet someone who will tell them about Jesus. Or we might pray that God will give them a meal or a warm place to sleep tonight. Even though we don't know the people who will get these bags, God already knows, and <u>he hears us</u> when we ask him to be with these people.**

Lead kids in praying for the people who will get the care kits. Invite each child to pray individually. If kids don't want to pray out loud, it's okay—they can have a moment to pray silently and specifically for the people who will get the bags they made.

Close in prayer, thanking God that <u>he hears us</u>.

Then say: **We can be sure that <u>God hears us</u> when we pray to him. He heard Hannah, and he hears every word you say to him, even if the words are just in your heart. <u>God hears us</u>, and he'll answer in one way or another!**

GOD'S ON MY SIDE!

BIBLE STORY: **David defeats Goliath.** *(1 Samuel 17)*

BIBLE POINT: <u>**God helps us do great things.**</u>

BIBLE VERSE: **"For I can do everything through Christ, who gives me strength"** *(Philippians 4:13)*.

Bible Insight

▸ By the time David killed Goliath, Samuel had already anointed David as Israel's next king. Unaware of this fact, Saul enlisted David to play his harp in Saul's court to fend off evil spirits (1 Samuel 16:15, 18). The Bible tells us that David pleased Saul, who loved him very much (1 Samuel 16:21).

▸ Saul eventually promoted David to serve as his armor bearer. This was an incredibly important position, given only to someone a king trusted completely. Armor bearers traditionally assisted the king as he went into battle, but these roles were reversed when Saul gave David his armor (which David chose not to use) and sent *him* into battle in the king's place.

▸ Samuel describes Saul as "head and shoulders taller than anyone else in the land" (1 Samuel 9:2). Therefore, Saul appeared to be the most logical person to fight Goliath and was possibly the target of Goliath's challenge. Yet David stepped up, acting like a king who fights for his country.

▸ A sling was a highly effective weapon in the ancient world. A projectile released from a sling could fly as fast as 150 miles per hour and hit a target 200 yards away. This allowed the shooter to attack from a safe distance. Soldiers considered aptitude with a sling a sign of military competence. David trusted in God, giving him an even more effective and powerful "weapon."

▸ For years, David had trained for his battle with Goliath without even knowing it. His seemingly menial job of caring for sheep gave him the opportunity to face fierce enemies, step out in courage, and remain vigilant. He learned how to fight something bigger than himself and trust in God's protection.

Kid Insight

Kids often compare themselves to others and feel like they don't have as much to offer. As the youngest of eight boys in the family, David probably felt that same way. Yet God chose David, not only to defeat Goliath but also to become Israel's leader. God looks for people who love him and are willing to obey—like David. Kids need to know that they don't have to be the smartest, fastest, or most popular kid on the block. God has great plans for their lives even now! He can give kids all they need to do great things if they're just willing to take that first step to trust and obey.

You'll need:

- [ ] kid-friendly Bible
- [ ] volunteer to play David
- [ ] Bible-times costume for David
- [ ] sling (you can use a sample of the craft)
- [ ] 5 colored pompoms
- [ ] 4x3-inch pieces of felt (1 per child)
- [ ] markers
- [ ] child-safe scissors
- [ ] 2-foot-long pieces of string (2 per child)
- [ ] stapler
- [ ] small scraps of paper (5 per child)
- [ ] pencils
- [ ] 2 trash cans
- [ ] disposable cups (1 for every 2 kids)
- [ ] pompoms (5 per child)
- [ ] "Philippians 4:13" handout (p. 80)
- [ ] *Friends With God Bible Lessons Music* CD and music player

> If you can't find a volunteer to play David, modify your script slightly and play the role yourself. You'll simply need to have kids close their eyes and put on their imaginations while *you* don the Bible-times costume. If you're female and are uncomfortable playing the part of a male character, tweak the script and play this as a bystander.

Getting Ready

Photocopy the "Philippians 4:13" handout (p. 80) on card stock. Cut apart the cards, making one verse card per child.

Friend-Maker Icebreaker *(10 minutes)*

STAND STRONG

Welcome kids and introduce yourself.

Say: **Today we're going to hear about someone who was really strong—almost like a superhero!** Ask:

💬 **Tell about the strongest person *you* know.**

Share an example of your own, then let kids share with a few friends around them.

Say: **Being strong can help you win in some sports or games. But sometimes being smart, being quick, or having good balance gives you a greater advantage. Let's see what you need most to win *this* game.**

Have each child find a partner of relatively equal size, and tell pairs to spread out throughout the room.

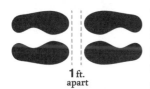

Tell kids to stand with their feet together, facing their partner, about a foot apart. Explain that the goal is to knock their partner off balance. They can do this by giving each other double high-fives until someone's feet move. They can touch the other person only on the hands and can't grab their hands and hold on. Ask another leader to help you demonstrate, if possible.

Have kids play for about a minute and then switch partners. Keep the energy high by playing an upbeat song such as "God Is for Me" from the *Friends With God Bible Lessons Music* CD.

After a few rounds, say: **We're going to change the rules a little bit. Now instead of battling your partner, you'll *team up* with your partner and challenge another pair.**

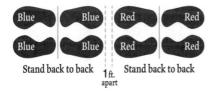

Have each pair find another pair to challenge. Determine which pair is Blue and which pair is Red. Direct Blues to stand back to back, facing Reds who are also back to back. With this setup, one Blue and one Red will be facing each other for the challenge, with their partners giving them support from behind. Have the Blue and Red challengers try to push each other off-balance, relying on the support from their partners (who cannot move). Then have partners switch roles and play again. Continue playing for a few minutes, then gather kids together.

> **Game Tip**
> You may want to have the "supporters" look down at their feet as they brace themselves to support the "challengers." This will keep kids from accidentally knocking heads with their partners.

Ask:

💬 **What skill was most important when you played on your own?**

💬 **How did that change when you had a partner behind you?**

💬 **Sometimes in real life, we need help or support. We even use the expression "I've got your back" to show that we're helping someone. Who is someone in real life who's got *your* back?**

Say: **Today we're going to meet someone who did some pretty amazing things. But he didn't do them alone. He had the greatest helper of all.**

Bible Adventure *(20 minutes)*

MEET DAVID

Place the sling and five colored pompoms where "David" can reach them. David should enter and begin a dialogue with kids. You may need to assist David. Join in the fun and surprise of talking with this friend of God!

(Creep in cautiously, then notice the kids.)

You kids don't look like you're from around here. You aren't Philistines, are you? *(Look at kids suspiciously.)* I'm looking for any Philistines left in the area. Have you seen any? *(Allow kids to respond.)* You don't seem like you've ever met a Philistine, and let me tell you, you don't really want to.

Sorry, let me introduce myself. My name's David, and I'm an Israelite. I actually haven't been involved in this battle—well, until today. I just arrived this morning to check on my older brothers. See, I'm the youngest in my family. It's not easy being the youngest in the family. *Ask:*

💬 How many of YOU are the youngest in your family?

So some of you know what I mean. While my older brothers get to go on exciting adventures, I get left behind doing the boring stuff like watching the sheep. Sheep don't do much; they just stand around eating grass all day long. I mean, sometimes a bear or a lion comes along and I have to fight it off. But most of the time, it's just BORING.

That's why I was excited when my dad asked me to take some bread and grain to my brothers. They're soldiers in Saul's army, facing our enemy, the PHILISTINES. The Philistines had been bragging about their fierce warrior named Goliath—he was taller than anyone we had ever seen. He was HUGE! Every day he challenged our mightiest fighters to a battle, but no one had the courage to face him. Even King Saul ran away from that big bully. *Ask:*

💬 Who's the scariest person you can think of?

Well, that's what my brothers faced every day! My dad loaded up the bread and grain and said, *(say this in a deeper, "Dad" voice)* "David, take this food to your brothers. Then come back here and tell me how they're doing." He sounded kinda worried about them.

When I got to my brothers, they were scared to death...and for good reason! Let me give you an idea of what was happening. *(Separate the class into two groups. Have the groups stand on opposite sides of the room, facing each other.)* Now you kids over here *(gesture to one side of the room)* are going to be the Philistines. Stomp around over here like giants, and let me see your meanest, scariest, biggest bully faces. *(Give kids a minute to stomp around like giants.)* Wow! You guys are pretty scary.

Now you kids over here *(gesture to the other side of the room)* are the Israelites. Show me what YOU would look like if you were really, REALLY scared of those Philistines over there. *(Look around.)* Yep, this is about what things looked like when I got to the camp. Every soldier in our army shook in his boots! For the 40th day in a row, a giant named Goliath bullied us and made fun of God. Philistines, why don't you all yell in your meanest voices, "Who can defeat me?" *(Give kids a minute to yell. Pretend to be a bit scared.)*

Okay, Israelites, show me what you think our army did. *(Let kids show you a response.)* Well, I'll tell you, our army just quivered in their boots. I couldn't believe it. I mean—we have GOD on our side! No one's stronger than GOD! I knew God would give us the strength to fight, even against a big, mean, mighty bully like Goliath!

So, I went straight to King Saul and told him I would fight Goliath. v

"Don't be ridiculous!" said Saul. "You're just a shrimpy kid. That bully will squash you like a bug! You're no match for a seasoned soldier like Goliath." Saul was right. (*Look down at yourself.*) I'm NOT very big. In fact, even King Saul's way bigger than I am. Maybe you've felt like that, too. *Ask:*

💬 Has anyone ever told you that you weren't big enough to do something? Tell a friend about it. (*Give kids a minute to share with a friend.*)

But I told Saul I didn't need to be afraid. I knew God was on our side. So Saul agreed to let me fight. He gave me his own heavy armor for protection, but it was WAY too big. Besides, I didn't need it. God would be my armor.

Now back when I watched the sheep, whenever I fought off wild animals, I used my trusty sling. So I grabbed my sling and a few smooth stones from the stream. (*Grab the sling and the pompoms.*) Then I marched out to face the giant. As I got closer, I could see that he was even gianter than I imagined. Still, I kept going.

Goliath laughed at me. He sneered at me. Goliath mocked me and told me he would feed me to the birds. Philistines, let me hear your meanest laugh. (*Give kids a minute to laugh.*) Now, Israelites, you're still just as scared. (*Encourage Israelites to continue to cower.*)

But I glared up at the giant and shouted, "You come to battle with your great big sword and spear, but I come to you in the name of the Lord, the God of Israel! He's the only weapon I need. I will beat you because this is the Lord's battle! Then everyone will know that the Lord rescues his people."

I put a stone in my sling and wound it up. (*Put a pompom in your sling.*) My sling twirled faster and faster, swish, swish, swish. (*Twirl the sling above your head.*) I let the stone fly (*release the pompom or just let the sling go limp*), and it smacked Goliath on the forehead. (*Smack your forehead.*) Philistines, do this with me... He wobbled. (*Encourage Philistines to wobble.*) He stumbled. (*Encourage Philistines to stumble.*) And then the giant fell face first into a dusty field. THUNK! (*Encourage Philistines to fall down—carefully.*)

For a long moment, nobody in either army moved. Or breathed. (*Encourage everyone to freeze.*) I walked forward (*take a few steps forward*), pulled out Goliath's own sword (*pretend to draw a sword*), and cut off his head! (*Pretend to hit the ground with the sword.*)

All right, Philistines, hop back up because then one Philistine soldier...and then another...and then the entire Philistine army turned tail and ran away like a flock of scared sheep. We had won!

Israelites, you just won the war! Go capture those Philistines! (*Encourage the Israelites to cheer and then chase the Philistines around the room until they "capture" them and gently lead them back to you.*)

I knew God was with me and God helps us do great things. God helped me defeat that giant bully. And now the whole world knows how powerful our God is. I don't imagine YOU'RE going to meet any giants this week, but God has great plans for you, too.

Well, I should get going. (*Look around.*) I don't think there are any Philistines left around here. Besides, the Israelites are celebrating God's victory over the Philistines, and I want to join the party!

(*Wave goodbye and exit.*)

FEAR SHOOTERS

Say: **David bravely faced Goliath, though he was probably a little afraid, too. But instead of running away or hiding like the rest of the Israelites, David chose to move forward in spite of his fear. Because he did, God was able to do something amazing in his life.** Ask:

💬 **What are some great things God might help you do?**

Give kids a minute to discuss with their friends. While kids are talking, give each of them a piece of felt, scissors, and two pieces of string.

Say: **With God's help, David defeated a giant—*that* was a great thing!** <u>God helps us do great things</u>, **too. Let's make a reminder that fear doesn't need to stop us, because we have God on our side.**

Help kids use scissors to cut a small hole in the center of both short sides of the felt, ½ inch from the edge. Then direct kids to cut a 1-inch slit in the center of each of the longer sides. Help them overlap the two sides of one slit by about ¼ inch and staple it in place. Tell kids to do the same on the other side. Have kids tie the string through the holes.

While kids are working, share these interesting facts about slings in battle:

▸ **A sling was an important weapon in Bible times, and having sling shooters in your army showed that your army was strong.**

▸ **Something shot from a sling could fly as fast as 150 miles per hour and hit a target as far away as 200 yards. That way the shooter could attack from a safe distance.**

Say: **Now think of some "giants" or hard things that you face.** Give kids a few examples, such as homework, challenges with friends, getting along with family members, and a bully at school. Share a couple of examples of your own. Then give each child five scraps of paper and a pencil. Encourage kids to write or draw some fears or "giants" on the papers and then crumple them up. Place trash cans on both ends of the room.

Say: **When we trust God, we don't have to be afraid. We know God's with us and will help us do great things. That can send our fears flying! Let's try that right now.**

Have each child place a paper wad in the felt sling. Kids can wrap one of the strings around a hand a couple of times and hold the other string in the same hand. Show kids how to pinch the paper in the sling with the other hand, hold it behind their shoulder, and pull the strings tight. Then they can let go of the sling and swing it forward while letting go of the loose string to let the paper wad fly. (Kids will want to swing the sling from one side of their body to the other. If they go around in circles, the two strings will get twisted, and the sling won't release properly.) Give kids some time to practice their aim as they try to get the paper into the trash cans.

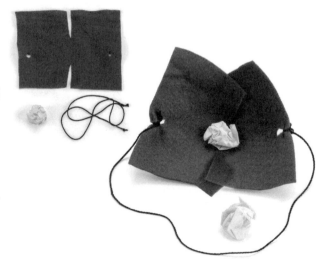

Say: **Even when we're afraid, we can always know that God's with us. And when God's with us,** <u>he helps us do great things</u>.

Have kids use their best dunk shot to put any remaining fear papers into the trash cans.

NICE SHOT!

Say: **David swung his sling around, and the rock flew right at Goliath's forehead. He never even had to get close to the giant. Let's practice hitting a target of our own.**

Have kids form pairs. Give one child in each pair a cup and the other child 10 pompoms. The partner with the cup will hold it on top of his or her head. The other partner will stand about 5 feet away and try to throw the pompoms into the cup. If they'd like, kids can also try to use their Fear Shooters to shoot the pompoms into the cups. Once all 10 pompoms are in the cup, the partners change roles. Alter the distance between partners as necessary to keep the game from being too hard or too easy for kids.

Say: **It took some practice to hit our targets. As a shepherd, David probably had lots of practice with his sling. But he probably never imagined he'd use that skill to kill a 9-foot giant! David needed more than practice—he needed God's help!** Ask:

💬 **What's something you could never do on your own?**

Start the discussion with something outrageous that you could never do, like fly to the moon or swim an ocean. Then let kids call out their own outrageous examples. Ask:

💬 **What help would you need to** [say some of the responses kids shared]?

Say: **God may not help us fly to the moon or swim the Atlantic Ocean. But God promises to help us when we feel overwhelmed. Listen to this.** Read aloud Philippians 4:13. Ask:

💬 **When would it comfort or encourage you to hear this verse? Why?**

Say: **God has awesome, unimaginable plans for you! If you knew today some of the plans God has for you, you might think, "No way!" But God promises to give us the strength we need to live out his plans.** <u>God helps us do great things.</u>

I Can Do All Things

Say: **God has great plans for each person he made. He gives us what we need to do anything he asks us to do. Remember, Philippians 4:13 says, "For I can do everything through Christ, who gives me strength."** Hand out a verse card and a pencil to each child.

Say: **The things God asks *us* to do may not feel *nearly* as important as defeating an army. But something as simple as a kind word to someone who's hurting can turn that person's whole week around. We never know what God's going to do through us. David didn't plan to defeat an army when he left home. He was just going to take some food to his brothers. But God had bigger plans.** Ask:

💬 **Think of one specific thing that seems kind of hard right now that you need God's help with.**

To help kids get started, share a way God might ask you to help someone. It could be to help a friend, tell a neighbor about Jesus, or volunteer at a homeless shelter. Then have kids write or draw on the back of their cards something God might want them to do. Point out that God may ask us to do something that seems small, like eat lunch with the kid at school who doesn't have any friends, practice soccer with a brother, or even tell someone about God's love for them.

Say: **Let's pray and ask God to help us do these hard things.**

Pray: **God, sometimes the things you ask us to do seem hard. Please help us remember that you help us do great things. Help us be willing to obey you. Hear us as we silently ask for your help with these great things.** Pause while kids pray silently, asking God to help them do the thing they wrote on their cards.

Continue praying: **God, thank you that you have a special plan for each one of our lives. We can't wait to see the great things you plan to do through each one of us. In Jesus' name, amen.**

Say: **Take these cards home and keep them handy this week. When something comes to mind that you could do to help someone or just to be kind to that person, remember that God helps us do great things.**

For I can do everything through Christ, who gives me strength.

(Philippians 4:13)

For I can do everything through Christ, who gives me strength.

(Philippians 4:13)

For I can do everything through Christ, who gives me strength.

(Philippians 4:13)

For I can do everything through Christ, who gives me strength.

(Philippians 4:13)

For I can do everything through Christ, who gives me strength.

(Philippians 4:13)

For I can do everything through Christ, who gives me strength.

(Philippians 4:13)

For I can do everything through Christ, who gives me strength.

(Philippians 4:13)

For I can do everything through Christ, who gives me strength.

(Philippians 4:13)

For I can do everything through Christ, who gives me strength.

(Philippians 4:13)

For I can do everything through Christ, who gives me strength.

(Philippians 4:13)

For I can do everything through Christ, who gives me strength.

(Philippians 4:13)

For I can do everything through Christ, who gives me strength.

(Philippians 4:13)

For I can do everything through Christ, who gives me strength.

(Philippians 4:13)

For I can do everything through Christ, who gives me strength.

(Philippians 4:13)

For I can do everything through Christ, who gives me strength.

(Philippians 4:13)

For I can do everything through Christ, who gives me strength.

(Philippians 4:13)

For I can do everything through Christ, who gives me strength.

(Philippians 4:13)

For I can do everything through Christ, who gives me strength.

(Philippians 4:13)

BIBLE STORY: **Abigail brings peace.** *(1 Samuel 25:2-38)*

BIBLE POINT: **God gives us wisdom.**

BIBLE VERSE: **"If you need wisdom, ask our generous God, and he will give it to you. He will not rebuke you for asking"** *(James 1:5).*

Bible Insight

▶ During his time on the run from King Saul, David lived as a fugitive, leading a band of outlaws. He spent this time protecting the people of Judah from invaders and thieves. He and his followers lived on a share of the crops, herds, and livestock he protected. David protected Nabal's livestock and servants. In fact, one of Nabal's servants describes David and his men as "a wall of protection to us and the sheep" (1 Samuel 25:16). In providing a valuable service to Nabal, David expected to be repaid for his trouble.

▶ It was appropriate for David to request compensation during sheepshearing time since during this festival season, workers received profits. Nabal insulted David with his rude response, as well as his refusal to give David anything.

▶ Abigail courageously rode alone into a group of 400 angry men. Her respectful and humble words helped defuse a tense situation. Abigail appealed to David on the basis of his faith, his reputation, and his legacy. It's interesting to note a similar bit of wisdom in Proverbs 20:22: "Don't say, 'I will get even for this wrong.' Wait for the Lord to handle the matter." This proverb is attributed to Solomon, David's son!

▶ The fact that Abigail could gather so much food so quickly is evidence of Nabal's wealth and how much he had to spare. Not only did she acknowledge David's service to her household by providing the bread, wine, and meat being served to the shearers, but she also added roasted grain, raisin clusters, and fig cakes. These traditional signs of hospitality during a festival season lasted a long time, so they would serve David and his men well.

Kid Insight

Kids' worlds are filled with conflict. Whether it's family conflict, disagreements with friends, or conflicts in the world around them, kids often feel powerless to avoid or resolve conflict. Kids need to know that God provides them with the wisdom to bring peace to the situations around them. God can give kids the wisdom they need to respond in a peaceful way to difficult circumstances, rather than just reacting in anger. When they do, others are likely to respond in a more agreeable way. While conflict will never be eliminated completely, life can certainly become more peaceful. Relying on God's wisdom, kids *can* find peace with their siblings, parents, and friends.

You'll need:

- ☐ kid-friendly Bible
- ☐ chair
- ☐ thin craft sticks or bamboo skewers (6 for every 4 or 5 kids)
- ☐ pennies (10 for every 4 or 5 kids)
- ☐ volunteer to play Abigail
- ☐ Bible-times costume for Abigail
- ☐ as many classroom items as possible to represent bread, meat, grain, raisins, and fig cakes (for example, small balls; paper plates; empty food containers; and bags of beads, popcorn, rice, or beans)
- ☐ 4 paper grocery bags
- ☐ cups (1 per person)
- ☐ 4 sheets of newsprint or bulletin board paper (each approximately 2x2 feet square)
- ☐ notecards or slips of paper (2 per child)
- ☐ pens or pencils
- ☐ crayons
- ☐ tape
- ☐ clear plastic plates (1 per child)
- ☐ permanent markers (various colors)
- ☐ curling ribbon (1-foot piece per child)
- ☐ *Friends With God Bible Lessons Music* CD and music player

> If you can't find a volunteer to play Abigail, modify your script slightly and play the role yourself. You'll simply need to have kids close their eyes and put on their imaginations while *you* don the Bible-times costume. If you're male, tweak the script and play this as David.

Getting Ready

Place the cups and the items representing the food in various places around the room. Put one of each item in a separate grocery bag, and put the bags within "Abigail's" reach.

Check out the "Brain Challenge Solutions" on page 90, and familiarize yourself with how to solve the puzzles.

Hang one large sheet of newsprint or bulletin board paper in each corner of the room, and set a handful of crayons nearby.

Friend-Maker Icebreaker *(10 minutes)*

BRAIN CHALLENGE

Welcome kids and introduce yourself.

Say: **There are a lot of questions in life that we have to answer. What do I want to eat for lunch? Which part of my homework should I do first? Which direction do I need to walk to find the bathroom? Here's a hint on that one: The bathroom's that way** (point to the bathrooms). **Some questions are easy to answer, and some really make us think.** Ask:

💬 **Tell a friend about a puzzle or problem that required you to use all your brain power to solve.**

Share your own example, such as doing a home repair or figuring out how to fit everyone around the table at Thanksgiving. Then give kids a minute to share with a friend sitting nearby.

Say: **Well, I'm glad you're all here today, because I have some puzzles for you to solve. You'll need your thinking caps and some help from your friends to find the solution.**

Have kids form groups of four or five, and give each group either a set of sticks or a set of pennies.

For kids with the sticks, explain that their goal is to figure out how to make six triangles that are all the same size using the six sticks. (They won't need to break the sticks.)

For kids with the pennies, show them how to put the pennies in a triangle: four on the bottom, three in the next row, two in the row above that, and one on top. Tell kids that their goal is to flip the triangle so it's upside down by moving only *three* pennies.

Play the *Friends With God Sing-Along Songs* CD for a few minutes while kids work together to find a solution. If a group figures out the solution, encourage them to keep it to themselves. Allow them to use the remaining time to try to find a solution to the other problem.

After a few minutes, say: **Those puzzles put our brain power to the test. In case you didn't get to see it, here's the solution.** If a group found the solution to the problem, let them share with the rest of the group. If not, show kids the solution yourself. Then give kids a chance to solve their own puzzle.

Say: **It was good to see so many of you working together to find the solution! Teamwork can be a *great* thing!** Ask:

💬 **Why were you glad to have others working with you on these puzzles?**

💬 **Were there times in your group when people had different—or even opposite—ideas of how to solve the problem? What did you do?**

Say: **God has given us all different abilities and ways of doing things. That can make it hard to work together. But if we're wise, we can find ways to get along with others. Sometimes that means we need to ask God for help because** God gives us wisdom. **Today we're going to meet someone who had the wisdom to make peace and saved a bunch of people's lives in the process.**

Collect the pennies and the sticks, and set them aside.

MEET ABIGAIL

Place bags containing food items within reach of "Abigail." Abigail should enter and begin a dialogue with kids. You may be needed to assist Abigail. Join in the fun and surprise of talking with this friend of God's!

(Enter and sit down in the chair as if exhausted.)

Whew, keeping the peace around here sure is a lot of work. *Ask:*

💬 Have you ever met anyone who's hard to get along with? I mean REALLY hard?

💬 Without naming any names, what's something people do that makes them hard to get along with?

(Give kids a chance to share with the group, then continue.)

Well, my name is Abigail, and my husband, Nabal *(pronounced NAY-bal)*, sounds like some of the people you know. He's not the nicest person in the world. To tell you the truth, he's a bit of a grump.

It's sheepshearing time, and a man named David helped us out. He and his small army kept our shepherds and workers safe out in the fields. So David sent 10 of his men with a message of peace and blessings to Nabal. They asked Nabal if he had any extra food and supplies he could let them have as a thank you for their work.

Now let's be clear, *(say in a loud whisper)* Nabal's really rich, and he has more than enough to spare! Plus, David's men had protected us.

Nabal didn't think so. *(Cross your arms over your chest, stubbornly.)* He refused to give them ANYTHING. Even worse, Nabal made fun of David's men and called them names. He even had a few nasty things to say about David. How rude! After David's men had helped keep Nabal's flocks safe, he chased them away. What a bully! *Ask:*

💬 Tell about a time you did something nice for someone and that person wasn't nice in return. *(Give kids a minute to share with a friend, and remind them not to use anyone's name.)*

One of our servants heard Nabal's rude words to David's men and rushed to tell me. I groaned when I heard the news. I could only imagine how David would respond. I mean, David was a powerful man, and his men had served us well.

Well, David was mad—fighting mad. He and 400 of his men grabbed their swords and marched off to kill Nabal and everyone on our farm. I had to do something, and fast. So I gathered some of my servants and told them to round up as much food as they could—bread *(hold up an item representing bread)*, meat *(hold up an item representing meat)*, grain *(hold up an item representing grain)*, raisins *(hold up an item representing raisins)*, fig cakes *(hold up an item representing fig cakes)*, and lots to drink *(hold up a cup)*. We really did have plenty to spare.

Why don't you help me gather supplies for David's men? But we have to do it quickly!

(Have kids quickly gather all the "food" supplies you placed around the room and place them in the grocery bags. When everything has been gathered, continue with the story.)

All right. *(Look around at everything kids have gathered.)* That will have to do. I loaded it up on some donkeys and raced out to meet David. Nabal had been wrong to not honor David's past kindness, and I wanted to make things right. I just hoped I wouldn't be too late.

As David and 400 soldiers neared my home, I met them on the road, with the mountains of food I'd brought with me. *(Gesture to the bags.)* I slipped off my donkey and knelt before David. *(Kneel.)* I apologized over and over for Nabal's terrible behavior, asking David not to settle the score by killing my husband and workers. I said, "Don't pay any attention to my husband. He's a fool! You're a good man, David. If you kill Nabal, it'll put a blemish on your record as a great man of God." *(Stand up.)*

That's when David realized what he'd been about to do. Was he really going to murder Nabal and his innocent workers because of an insult? *(Pause.)* Yes—until I caused David to pause, calm down, and see things clearly. *Ask:*

💬 **What helps you calm down when you're angry?**

💬 **What are ways you've helped someone else calm down?**

(Give kids a minute to talk with a few friends, and then continue.)

David nodded and said, "Wow, I think you're right. Thank you for bringing me to my senses! I HAD gotten pretty angry, and I'm glad you helped me calm down." Then he sent me home in peace.

(Flop back into your chair, exhausted.) **God gave me the wisdom to know how to make peace with David before many people got hurt. <u>God gives us all wisdom</u> if we ask him. He can help us all be peacemakers.**

Well, I need to get back home and check on things. Who KNOWS what Nabal's done now?

(Wave goodbye and exit.)

FEEDING FRIENDZEE

Say: **Abigail had to get *a lot* of food ready for all those soldiers, and she had to do it fast. It took wisdom— and a lot of help—to pull that off! Let's play a game where we have to get ready for a fast feast. First, let's think of what *you'd* want to eat at a feast.**

Hand each person two notecards or slips of paper and a pen or pencil. Have kids clearly write on each notecard something *they'd* want to eat at a feast. Then have kids fold their notecards so no one can see what they wrote. Gather the notecards in a paper grocery bag from the Bible Adventure, and place the bag in the center of the room.

Form four teams, and send each team to a different corner of the room to gather around the sheet of paper on the wall. Have each team designate the first "Artist."

Explain that when you say "go," one person will run to the bag, pull out a notecard, and silently read what's on it. Then he or she must return to his or her corner and silently act out the item for the Artist to draw as part of the feast. When the Artist has finished (and drawn the correct item), the person who acted out the food item will become the next Artist and another child will run and get a notecard. Teams will continue until each person has had a chance to draw *and* act. Then kids should sit down.

Play "God Will Guide Us" from the *Friends With God Bible Lessons Music* CD while kids play. When all teams are seated, take a look at the "feasts" they drew. Compliment kids on a tasty—and interesting—array of food! Gather the teams together, then ask:

💬 **Think about when you were the Artist. How did people let you know the right thing to draw?**

💬 **Brainstorm other ways people could've let you know what to draw.**

Kids might say things such as showing the written words, telling the Artist, or using other words to describe the food.

Say: **In real life, sometimes you're like the Artist, figuring out the right thing to do.** Ask:

💬 **Who gives you wisdom in life? How?**

Say: **You may be blessed to have wise friends or family or teachers who can help you out. But *everyone* has access to the ultimate source of wisdom. Listen to this.** Read aloud James 1:5. Ask:

💬 **Brainstorm some ways God gives you wisdom.**

If kids struggle, share a personal example about how God gave you wisdom, such as providing guidance through a wise friend or a Scripture that made things clear. Welcome kids' responses, and get them thinking about all the ways God speaks to us today.

Say: **Sometimes God speaks to our hearts, and sometimes he shows us things in nature. Other times, a piece of Scripture lets us know what to do. But whenever you ask, you can trust that <u>God gives us wisdom</u>.**

Sensible Servers

Say: **The Bible doesn't say that Abigail stopped and asked God for wisdom. But listen to how she's described.** Read aloud 1 Samuel 25:3, 32-33. Ask:

💬 **What does it mean to be sensible or have good sense?**

Say: **God had given Abigail a wise and sensible heart. She knew what to do and when to do it!** Ask:

💬 **Why was serving David a wise move?**

Say: **When Abigail served David and his men some food, that helped soothe David's anger. Let's make something to help us remember to be sensible and use the wisdom God gives as we serve others.**

Give each child a clear plastic plate, and set out permanent markers. Encourage kids to color the underside of their plates so their designs show through the top. After seven or eight minutes, make sure kids have their names on their plates, and have them set the crafts aside.

Say: **When you go home, you can use your plate to serve food to others. You can even wash the plate with dish soap so it can be used again and again. Just don't put it in the dishwasher.** Ask:

💬 **What are some ways you can serve or help others?**

💬 **Think of something you'd do to help your mom.** Pause. **How is that different from what you'd do to serve your best friend?**

Have kids share their answers with a few friends seated nearby. After a minute or two, take a few responses from anyone willing to share with the larger group.

Say: **Sometimes it can be hard to know the best way to help those around us. Each person is different and responds differently to different types of service. God gave Abigail the wisdom and sense to know how to best meet the needs of David and his men. <u>God gives us wisdom</u>, too, so we can know the best way to reach out with his love.**

TIED IN KNOTS

Say: **When we're not sure what to do, our hearts can feel tied up in knots. Let's see what that's like.**

Give each child a piece of ribbon. Show kids how to tie a slipknot.

▸ Make a loop at one end of the ribbon, crossing one side of the ribbon over the other. Hold this in place with one hand.

▸ Pull a section of the ribbon that's on top back under your hand (that's on the bottom) and up through the loop. This forms another loop.

▸ Pull the new loop tight.

Say: **Sometimes we have a hard time getting along with someone. We get all tied up and don't know what to do.** Ask:

💬 **Think of someone you've had a hard time getting along with recently.**

Give kids a minute to think, and then say: **If we fight to get our own way, it's like pulling on *this* ribbon.** Direct kids to hold on to the loop with one hand and pull the left side of the ribbon with the other hand. **It only makes things worse, just like our knot getting tighter. But God promises to give us wisdom if we ask him.** Read aloud James 1:5 from a kid-friendly Bible translation.

Say: <u>God gives us the wisdom</u> **to see what someone else might be thinking or feeling, like he did for Abigail. If we can look at things someone else's way, it's like pulling on the other ribbon** (show kids how to pull the right-side ribbon to untie the knot), **and the fight can end, like it did for David. Let's pray and ask God for his wisdom to help us be at peace with others.**

Pray: **God, give us the wisdom to see what might help us get along with others. Help us not to respond in anger when we're hurt but to trust you.**

Give kids a chance to pray silently for the situations they thought about earlier. Encourage them to ask God for the wisdom to see what the other person might be feeling.

Continue praying: **God, help us when we have trouble getting along with others. Give us wisdom to try to understand other people's point of view and help them get what they need. We want to live at peace. In Jesus' name, amen.**

Brain Challenge Solutions

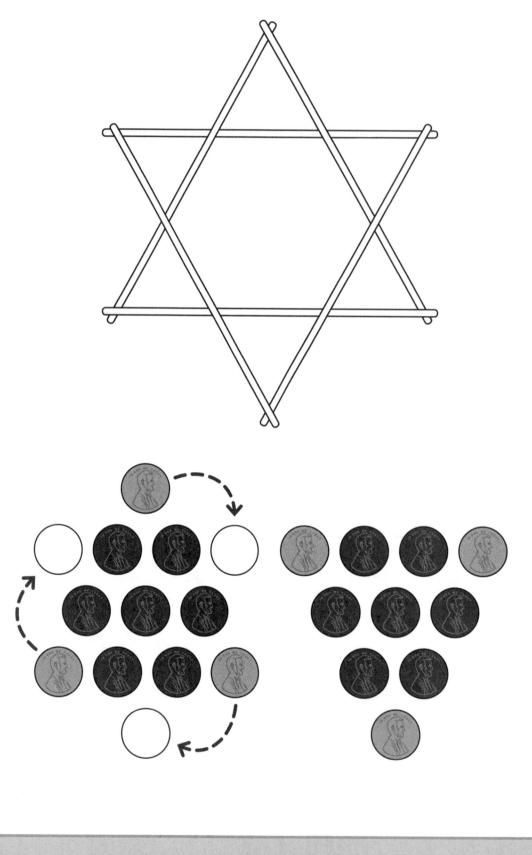

As Real As It Gets

BIBLE STORY: **Elijah confronts the prophets of Baal.** *(1 Kings 18:1-40)*

BIBLE POINT: **God is powerful.**

BIBLE VERSE: **"How great is our Lord! His power is absolute! His understanding is beyond comprehension!"** *(Psalm 147:5)*.

Bible Insight

▸ King Ahab ruled about 150 years after David, and by that time, the northern kingdom of Israel was practicing the same idolatry that the Israelites supposedly detested. With Queen Jezebel, he promoted the worship of the false god Baal and "did more to provoke the anger of the Lord, the God of Israel, than any of the other kings of Israel before him" (1 Kings 16:33). When Elijah opposed this pagan worship, Ahab labeled him the "troublemaker of Israel" (1 Kings 18:17).

▸ The New Testament states that no rain fell "for three and a half years" (James 5:17). The early rain in the region fell in what would be our spring season, and the latter rain fell in our fall. Though Ahab might have at first dismissed Elijah's pronouncement, when neither of these rains fell at their normal times, he became obsessed with finding the prophet, searching "every nation and kingdom on earth from end to end" (1 Kings 18:10).

▸ Mount Carmel is a high bluff that extends from the western coast of Israel toward the southeast. The spot where the contest between Elijah and the prophets of Baal took place is situated at the eastern end, which is also the highest point of the ridge. The spot was perfectly situated for the thousands of Israelites to have a good view of the action. The summit, 1,635 feet above the sea, on which the altars were placed, provided ample space for the king and the priests of Baal to stand on one side and Elijah on the other.

Kid Insight

In our society, kids are surrounded by relativism. With relativism, there are no absolutes—truth depends solely on your point of view. Maybe God is real; maybe he's not. Maybe there's life after death; maybe nothing happens when we die. Maybe Jesus is the only way to heaven; maybe all religions get you there. Your kids have probably heard these—and many more—relative points of view. So to ground them in the knowledge that our amazing God is the one and only true God is more than important—it's imperative. When kids realize that God is all-knowing and all-powerful, they can count on him with complete confidence. Use this Bible story to help your kids realize that this powerful God who Elijah called on is the same God they can call on today. The same God who blasted the altar with fire is the same God who listens to their scared prayers at night. He's the same God who cares deeply about them. And he's the same loving God who longs for an eternal friendship with them.

You'll need:

- ☐ kid-friendly Bible
- ☐ inflatable beach balls (1 for every 8-10 kids)
- ☐ permanent marker
- ☐ volunteer to play Elijah
- ☐ Bible-times costume for Elijah
- ☐ chenille wires (at least 8 per child)
- ☐ small pompoms (enough to fill 2 large bowls)
- ☐ 4 large bowls
- ☐ plastic spoons
- ☐ craft sticks (at least 16 per child, plus 16 for you)
- ☐ red cellophane
- ☐ scissors
- ☐ Glue Dots
- ☐ fine-tipped markers (1 per child)
- ☐ *Friends With God Bible Lessons Music* CD and music player

> If you can't find a volunteer to play Elijah, modify your script slightly and play the role yourself. You'll simply need to have kids close their eyes and put on their imaginations while *you* don the Bible-times costume. If you're female, tweak the script and play this as a friend of Elijah.

Getting Ready

Prepare one or more beach balls for the opening activity. You'll need one beach ball for every eight to 10 kids. Inflate a beach ball and use a permanent marker to write a different get-to-know-you question in each of the ball's panels. You might write questions such as "What's your favorite thing to do on the weekend?" and "If you could travel anywhere in the world, where would you go?" and "Who's your favorite cartoon character?"

Also, create a sample craft to show kids. Follow the directions in the "Altar Altercations" section.

> You can purchase a Throw & Tell Ball covered with engaging, surprising, and fun-to-answer questions from Group Publishing or your local Group supplier.

THE LESSON

Friend-Maker Icebreaker *(10 minutes)*

BEACH BALL BONANZA

Welcome kids and introduce yourself.

Say: **Here at** [name of your church], **it's fun to make new friends and play with old ones. Before we jump in to our first activity, I have a quick question for you.** Ask:

💬 **What do you like to do with a friend? Do you have a favorite game? a favorite place to go?**

Give your own example first, sharing about a favorite activity you like to do with a friend or family member. (Be sure to remind kids that family members *can* be friends, too!) Then let kids share with someone sitting nearby.

Say: **It sounds like you have a lot of fun with your friends! I'm glad! Let's play a game that will give us a chance to have fun *and* get to know each other better.**

Form groups of eight to 10 kids, and have kids in each group stand in a circle facing in. Give each group a prepared beach ball. When you give the signal, the first child in each group will bop the beach ball across the circle. The child who catches the ball will read aloud the question on the panel facing him or her and then answer it so everyone can hear. Then that child will bop the ball to another person, who will read and answer a question. Continue play until each person in the circle has answered a few questions.

Play "My God Is Powerful" from the *Friends With God Bible Lessons Music* CD softly in the background as kids bat the ball around. After about five minutes, turn off the music and have kids sit down. Ask:

💬 **What question was the hardest for you to answer? the easiest?**

💬 **What fun information did you learn about your friends?**

Say: **In real life, we usually don't throw a ball with questions on it at someone we want to be friends with. Becoming friends takes a little more time than that.** Ask:

💬 **How *do* you get to know new friends in real life?**

Say: **People usually become friends as they spend time together, talk to each other, and listen to each other. You know, it's kind of the same when we become friends with God—only way better! We can become friends with God by spending time reading his book, the Bible. And we can talk to him and listen for him to talk to us.**

Being friends with God is amazing because, unlike our regular friends, he's *God*! He knows everything, he can be everywhere, and he's more powerful than anything. Not only that, but he loves us! Think about that—the Creator of the universe, the Creator of everything and everyone, loves you and wants to be your friend! That's a pretty good friend to have, don't you think?

Let's meet a guy from the Bible who discovered just how amazing it was to have our awesome, powerful God as his friend!

Place the beach balls out of sight.

Meet Elijah

Place the chenille wires where "Elijah" can reach them. Elijah should enter and begin a dialogue with kids. You may be needed to assist Elijah with props or lighting. Join in the fun and surprise of talking with this friend of God!

(Enter and slowly walk around the room while speaking.)

Some people have a hard time believing God loves them.

But not me! *(Point proudly to yourself.)* My name is Elijah, and God has taken care of me through some really hard times. Maybe you know what that's like. *Ask:*

💬 When has God been with you during a hard time? *(Have kids form trios, and allow time for discussion, making sure each person has a chance to share.)*

God is powerful, and his power comes in all shapes and sizes. That reminds me that I found these fun, twisty things that make all kinds of shapes. *(Hand each person a chenille wire.)* Let's use these to help you understand how God's power took shape in my life!

Even when I was hiding from mean King Ahab in the desert, God sent ravens to bring me food every day. Ravens are birds, kind of like crows. To think God showed his love for me through birds! Can you bend your wire into a bird shape? *(Have kids each create a bird shape with the wire.)* What a cool reminder of God's love and provision.

I couldn't avoid Ahab forever, though. Even though that troublemaker wanted to kill me, God sent me to prove to Ahab that God is real—and that his fake gods were, well, fake.

I met Ahab on Mount Carmel for a major showdown. *(Have kids each make a mountain shape with the wire.)* He brought 450 of his prophets of Baal. Baal was the fake god Ahab chose to follow instead of the one true God. I told Ahab's prophets to build an altar to Baal while I built my own altar to God. *(Encourage kids to each make an altar shape with the wire. Explain that in this case, the altar was a kind of wooden platform.)*

"The god who brings fire to an altar is the one true God!" I said. "If Baal is God, then follow him. But if the Lord is God, then you must follow him!"

Those poor prophets of Baal tried and tried and tried and tried to get Baal to send fire. They danced and hollered like a bunch of fools. I told them to yell louder, but it didn't help. Baal was fake—he had no power at all.

I poked fun at them because I knew nothing would happen. I said, "Maybe Baal went on vacation! Maybe he's asleep! Maybe he's out going to the bathroom!" *(Have kids make a smile shape with the wire to show that you were laughing at the prophets of Baal.)*

Then it was my turn. Drumroll, please. *(Lead kids in patting their legs in a drumroll for a few seconds.)*

I had all the people gather around close so they could see what I was doing. I had them pour 12 big jugs of water all over my altar. It was soaked! *(Have kids use the wire to each make a shape that suggests water—a water drop, a water jug, or even waves.)*

Then I stood before my altar and simply prayed *(bow your head)*, "God, show these people that you're really there. Show them your power. Prove to them that you are the ONE TRUE GOD."

No sooner had I spoken than a flash of fire blazed out of the sky. In an instant, it burned my altar to a crisp. Everything in it was burned to ashes—even the rocks! No one could deny that God is powerful! *(Let kids use the wire to make a shape that suggests fire or flames.)*

Needless to say, everyone was amazed. The people dropped to the ground and cried, "Yes! The Lord—he is God! Yes, the Lord is God!"

Yes! Yes, he is. The people saw God's power and finally believed in him!

Now you probably won't ever see a spectacular sight like fire falling from heaven. *(Point to kids in turn as you speak.)* But because God honors his friends who believe in him without ever seeing dazzling miracles, that makes you special. YOU can help other people believe in God and his power! *Ask:*

💬 Who in your life needs to know that God is powerful?

💬 What can you do to help that person know God and recognize his power?

Having faith means trusting God even though you can't see him standing in front of you. And sharing that faith is super important. Because God is real! And God really loves you! He cares about what's going on in your life, and he'll help you through every situation— just like he helped me! *Ask:*

💬 What's a situation in your life right now where you need God's power to help you?
   (Have kids discuss the question in their trios for about a minute.)

God is powerful. If you look, you can see God's power at work in the world all around you. Kind of like the ravens took care of me, think of all the ways God has provided for your needs, kept you safe, and brought loving people into your life.

Well, the life of a prophet is busy—God ALWAYS has something new to say. So I'd better leave. Thanks for letting me share my story!

(Wave and exit.)

(Have the leader collect the chenille wires for use later in the Creation Station.)

RAVEN RELAY

Say: <u>God is powerful</u> in so many ways. Listen to this verse about God's power. Read aloud Psalm 147:4. Ask:

💬 **What does this passage tell you about God's power?**

Say: **In today's Bible story, we saw God's power in a big way against the prophets of Baal. But God uses his power in smaller ways, too, like when he sent ravens to take food to Elijah. Let's play a game called Raven Relay to help us remember that God can use his power in all kinds of surprising ways!**

Form two teams of equal number, and have teams line up at one end of the room. Give each team a supply of plastic spoons and a large bowl of small pompoms. Set out another large bowl for each team at the other end of the room.

Say: **Each of you is going to be a raven that takes food across the room for Elijah. When it's your turn, place the handle of a plastic spoon in your mouth, and dip the spoon in the bowl to scoop up a pompom. Then "fly" across the room, drop the food into the bowl, and fly back. There's no running—all you ravens need to walk heel-to-toe.**

Give a starting signal and let the ravens race! After the first round, play several more times, changing the way the ravens move. You might have them hop, scissor-step, or crawl. After the game, let everyone sit to rest. Ask:

💬 **Which way that the ravens moved in our game was your favorite? Why?**

💬 **God could have made food just appear; why do you think he used ravens to take food to Elijah?**

💬 **When is a time in your life you saw God provide for you or your family?**

Say: <u>God is powerful</u>, and he shows his power and love for us in both big and small ways. I just love that about God! Right now, let's make something to help us remember God's awesome power!

ALTAR ALTERCATIONS

Set out craft sticks, chenille wires, Glue Dots, red cellophane, and scissors. Show kids the sample Altar Altercation you made earlier.

Say: **Today we're going to make what I call Altar Altercations!** Hold up the sample altar you made for everyone to see. **An *altercation* is defined as a "noisy quarrel." That's a perfect description of what happened on Mount Carmel with Elijah and the prophets of Baal, wouldn't you say? These Altar Altercations can remind us that <u>God is powerful</u> today, just as he was a long time ago with Elijah!**

You can lead kids through the following simple steps or let them create their altars any way they choose. Just remind them to leave room to add the red cellophane on the top of the altar.

1. Place four craft sticks side by side.

2. Weave a chenille wire over and under the sticks to lash them together near the top of the sticks. Leave a little room between the sticks.

3. Use another chenille wire to connect the sticks near the bottom. The sticks will look a little like a raft.

4. Repeat steps 1-3 to make another layer of sticks. Use Glue Dots to stick the layers together (like a layer cake).

5. Continue until you have at least four layers. This is your altar.

6. Cut a small piece of red cellophane, about 3x4 inches, to represent fire. Twist one corner of the cellophane, and use a Glue Dot to attach it to the top layer of the altar.

Say: **Your Altar Altercations are looking good! You can take your craft home and use it to tell your family what happened when Elijah took on the prophets of Baal. Elijah knew that <u>God is powerful</u>, and our altars can help us remember that, too!**

Have kids help clean up and put craft supplies away.

POWER PRAYERS

Have kids sit in a circle with their Altar Altercations. Set out fine-tipped markers.

Say: **Today we explored a cool example of God's power. But, you know, God is still powerful today! He's always at work in our lives, and he shows his power and love in both big and small ways.**

Earlier, during our Bible story, you thought of a situation in your life right now where you need God's power. Use a marker to write on your altar a word or two that represents that situation. You might write "forgiveness" or "sickness" or "protection." If you have more than one situation where you need God's power in your life, write words to represent each situation. Give kids time to write on their altars.

After kids finish writing, have them hold their altars in their hands while you pray.

Pray: **Dear God, we're amazed by your awesome power. And we thank you for using your power to help us. Please be with each of us in the specific situations we're bringing before you. Thank you for always hearing us and for always loving us. In Jesus' name we pray, amen.**

Have kids take their altars home as reminders that <u>God is powerful</u>. Encourage kids to use their altars to tell family members and friends about God's amazing power.

Let It Flow, Let It Flow, Let It Flow

BIBLE STORY: **Elisha provides for a widow.** *(2 Kings 4:1-7)*

BIBLE POINT: **God gives us what we need.**

BIBLE VERSE: "Now all glory to God, who is able, through his mighty power at work within us, to accomplish infinitely more than we might ask or think" *(Ephesians 3:20).*

Bible Insight

▶ After the division of Israel into two kingdoms, people displayed general indifference toward spiritual subjects, especially in the northern kingdom. During this time, men who maintained their faith in God formed study groups called "companies of prophets" to keep knowledge of the Lord alive. While not official prophets appointed by God, men in these study groups followed God. The widow's husband had been a member of one of these "groups of prophets." Both Elisha and Elijah before him were in close relationship with the members of these groups.

▶ Mosaic law (Leviticus 25:39-41) stated that a debtor might be taken as a servant by a creditor and his debt canceled by his labor. In this case, the debtor was dead, but his children could still be taken. The law also stated that they could go free in the Year of Jubilee.

▶ It must have tested the widow's faith to be told to gather so many empty jars—what use could she possibly have for empty containers when all she had was one jar of oil herself? But having been the wife of a man who feared the Lord, perhaps she had come to know that God could be counted on for help and sustenance. It's interesting that Elisha told the woman that after she collected all the empty jars possible, she and her sons must go in the house and shut the door. This miracle would be performed in private.

Kid Insight

Kids often feel helpless and inadequate. They're not old enough to earn money, other than perhaps a weekly allowance. They generally can't make important decisions in their families or schools. They don't feel as if they have much control in their lives. Add to that thoughts of inferiority that kids often have—I'm not good at sports, I'm not smart, I'm not good-looking, I don't have the same "stuff" that other kids have—and kids may feel deficient. Use this lesson to help kids know that no matter what their worldly circumstances, they can have an abundance of a highly important commodity—faith in God! Just as God used the widow's small amount of oil in a miraculous way, God can use a child's faith and grow it into a mighty and powerful tool!

You'll need:

- ☐ kid-friendly Bible
- ☐ volunteer to play Elisha
- ☐ Bible-times costume for Elisha
- ☐ small plastic containers with lids, roughly 3 ounces each (2 per person) (dollar discount stores typically sell 4-6 in a pack)
- ☐ 20 or more ads for local services (such as those that come with newspapers, in the mail as local marketing packets, or at grocery stores)
- ☐ permanent markers in a variety of colors
- ☐ olive oil (1 tablespoon per child)
- ☐ granulated sugar (¼ cup per child)
- ☐ measuring cups
- ☐ measuring spoons
- ☐ spoons
- ☐ essential oils (optional)
- ☐ paper
- ☐ pens
- ☐ *Friends With God Bible Lessons Music* CD and music player

> If you can't find a volunteer to play Elisha, modify your script slightly and play the role yourself. You'll simply need to have kids close their eyes and put on their imaginations while *you* don the Bible-times costume. If you're female, tweak the script and play this as a friend of Elisha.

Getting Ready

Make a sample Scratchy Scrub to show kids. Decide on a homeless shelter or safe house to donate the scrubs to.

❈ THE LESSON ❈

WHATCHA GOT?

Welcome kids and introduce yourself.

Say: **We've all come together to dig into an amazing, unbelievable—but totally true—Bible story about a time God provided something that someone desperately needed. That has me wondering if *you* have what you need for this game. We'll find out!**

Form teams of four, and have teams scatter around the room and sit down. Explain that this is a one-room scavenger hunt. You'll call out an item, and kids will have to work with their team to bring it to you. Call out the following things (some are silly!), and give kids a chance to work on their solutions and see if they can bring the item to you as quickly as possible. When kids bring you something, give them a high-five. Point out that kids can use only what they have in their team—no additional classroom supplies.

- ▸ Three shoelaces tied together
- ▸ Two team members carrying a third team member
- ▸ An eight-legged creature (Kids can join together, since as a group they have eight legs.)
- ▸ A gum or candy wrapper
- ▸ Someone wearing a T-shirt with a word on it
- ▸ The word *sing* (Kids might point to it in a Bible or church bulletin or on a piece of clothing, or they might spell it out in sign language. Allow them to be creative!)
- ▸ A bookmark
- ▸ A picture of a president (See if kids have any coins or dollars with them.)

After the game, gather kids and sit in a circle. ("Elisha" will need kids in a circle when he comes to visit.) Ask:

- 💬 **What were some things you needed but didn't have?**
- 💬 **How did you feel when you didn't have the item I asked for?**
- 💬 **Think of something you really and truly need at home. Who provides that for you?**

Say: **We all need things like food and water, but we also need friendship, safety, comfort, and laughter. It doesn't feel good to miss out on those things! Today we'll explore how <u>God gives us what we need</u>. The Bible tells us that God provides an abundance—even *more* than we ask for or need!**

Read aloud Ephesians 3:20. Say: **Let's meet someone from the Bible who discovered firsthand that <u>God gives us what we need</u>.**

Meet Elisha

Place the plastic containers within reach of "Elisha." Elisha should enter and begin a dialogue with kids. You may be needed to assist with props or lighting. Join in the fun and surprise of talking with this friend of God!

Let It Flow, Let It Flow, Let It Flow

(Enter and excitedly talk to kids as you move around the room.)

I think God kind of likes surprises. You never know what creative new way God is going to use to give you what you need!

My name's Elisha, and I'm a prophet. That means I give people special, important messages from God. And believe me—God is ALWAYS surprising me!

Take this poor widow I just met. Her husband died and left her with a pile of debt. That means she owed a lot of money. The banker wanted his money. Soon he even threatened to take away her two sons and sell them as slaves if she didn't pay. But she was broke. All she had was one little jar of olive oil. *Ask:*

💬 When is a time you or your family needed God to provide for you? Maybe your mom or dad lost a job and money was tight, or maybe you needed a new house. *(Have kids form pairs, and allow time for discussion, making sure each partner has a chance to share.)*

We all run into trouble in our lives. And we all need God's help. If there's one thing I've learned, it's that <u>God gives us what we need</u>. He doesn't always give us what we THINK we need. And he doesn't always give us what we WANT. Those are whole different issues. But God ALWAYS knows what we need, and he's ALWAYS generous and giving.

Anyway, back to this poor widow I was telling you about.

Like I said, she had only one small jar of olive oil. *(Hand a child one of the plastic containers.)* She knew I talked to God a lot, so she asked me for help. And I knew God would come to her rescue.

I told her to borrow as many jars as she could find, from friends, neighbors, anyone who had an extra jar or two sitting around. *(Hand the same child another plastic container, then another and another, until you've piled all the plastic containers in the child's hands.)* **Then I told her to pour the oil from her one jar into all the empty jars.** *(Have the child start passing the plastic containers to the next child, and so on, until the all the containers are being passed around the circle.)*

She poured. And poured. And poured. And poured. And poured. *(Encourage kids to pass the containers faster and faster.)* **Her boys kept bringing her more and more jars, and her one little jar of oil filled every container to the brim.** *(Encourage kids to pass the containers as quickly as they can—faster and faster!)* **The oil kept flowing, and the widow kept pouring. It was a miracle! Oh, wait—you'd better stop passing those containers!**

(Have the leader collect all the containers except one and set them out of sight.)

"Now you and your sons can sell the oil and pay your debts," I told the widow. "You'll even have some money left over to live on!"

God could have met her needs in a hundred different ways. But he surprised her with more than she ever expected!

Don't you love happy endings? *(Hold up one of the containers.)* That one little jar of oil turned into a fountain of joy for that poor widow and her boys.

God's love works the same way! God keeps pouring his love into your life, and it never runs out. God met that widow's needs, and God meets your needs, too. *Ask:*

💬 **What needs do you have in your family right now? Talk with a partner.**
(Allow time for discussion.)

We all have needs, and we can always pray and ask God for help. You might be surprised by what God does! I'd like to pray for you right now.

(Lead kids in prayer.) **God, I know how much you love everyone here. You know everything they need. Please be with them and their families. Please give them what they need and then shower them with blessings, like you did for that widow. Thank you, God! In Jesus' name, amen.**

AD DASH

Look through the ads you'll be using to make sure there aren't any that are inappropriate for kids to see at church. Spread out the ads in a loose pile in the center of your room.

Say: **We've been exploring how** <u>God gives us what we need</u>. **Sometimes God provides for us through the help of other people. I have a bunch of advertisements here** (point to the pile of ads) **that have information about people and places in our community that could help with all kinds of needs. I'll call out a need, such as "I'm hungry!" The first person to bring me an ad that could help me with my need wins that round. Then I'll call out another need. We'll be playing fast, so listen carefully and move quickly.**

Have kids move to one side of the room, and you'll go to the other side, with the pile of ads between you and the kids. Call out the categories of needs listed below or any others you think of based on your assortment of ads. After a child brings you a suitable ad, quickly call out the next need so the game stays high-energy and fast-moving.

- ▸ **I'm thirsty!**
- ▸ **My car won't start!**
- ▸ **My pet is out of food!**
- ▸ **I'm hungry!**
- ▸ **I need a haircut!**
- ▸ **My shoes are full of holes!**
- ▸ **I need new clothes!**
- ▸ **I want a sandwich!**
- ▸ **My computer broke!**
- ▸ **I need a gift for my mom!**
- ▸ **I'm craving pizza!**
- ▸ **I'm cold!**
- ▸ **I'm too hot!**
- ▸ **I need to fix my house!**
- ▸ **I have a cavity in my tooth!**

After calling out the last need, have everyone gather around you and sit in a circle. Spread out the ads that were brought to you so everyone can see them.

Say: **Some of the things I called out were needs, and some were just wants—things I could live without.** Ask:

- 💬 **How did you decide what I needed in each situation?**
- 💬 **How can you tell when someone in real life needs your help?**
- 💬 **What sometimes keeps you from reaching out to help someone?**

Say: **In our Bible story, God used Elisha to help a widow in need. Sometimes God might even use *you* to give people what they need. Our game was just pretend, but when we have needs in real life, God can send people to help us.** <u>God gives us what we need</u>!

SCRATCHY SCRUBS

Ask:

💬 **When have you or your family helped someone in need?**

💬 **How does it feel to give something to people in need?**

Say: **In the Bible, God used Elisha to help provide what the widow needed. And today God can use *you* to help provide for people. You know, there are people right here in our community who might need some love and comfort in their lives. We can give them something they need.** Tell kids about the organization you'll be donating the Scratchy Scrubs to.

Give each child a plastic container, and set out permanent markers, olive oil, granulated sugar, measuring cups and spoons, and essential oils (if using). Have kids follow these directions to make Scratchy Scrubs.

▸ **Decorate the container with permanent markers.**

▸ **Pour ¼ cup of granulated sugar into the container.**

▸ **Pour 1 tablespoon of olive oil into the container.**

▸ **If using essential oils, add about two drops.**

▸ **Mix thoroughly; add more olive oil in small amounts if needed. Avoid making the scrub appear runny.**

While kids create, play "Pray About Everything" from the *Friends With God Bible Lessons Music* CD. When everyone has finished making a scrub, say: **In the Bible, the widow had only a little oil, but God gave her enough to fill many jars. We used oil to provide something else people need—clean hands! People can wash their hands with our scrubs to make their hands soft and clean. Our scrubs will give people something a little fancy and nice that they might not otherwise have.**

If it's practical, take your sample container to a sink and let kids take turns washing their hands with the scrub. Let kids help put away the supplies and clean up.

FILLED WITH THANKS

Say: **Today we explored an amazing example of God's love and generosity. He gave the widow not only what she needed but also far more than she ever could have imagined! That reminds me of this verse.**

Read aloud Ephesians 3:20.

Say: **God doesn't give us only physical things. He also gives us things we can't see, like confidence, faith, and the strength to get through hard times.** Ask:

💬 **What's an area of your life right now where you need God to give you something you can't see?**

Have kids discuss the question in trios. After discussion, invite a few willing kids to share their thoughts with the whole group. Then distribute paper, pens, and plastic containers.

Say: **God is so loving and good. <u>God gives us what we need</u>. But sometimes we focus on what we *still* need rather than on what God has already given us. Let's thank God for giving us what we need. Think of things God has given that you're thankful for. Think of things you can see and things you can't see.**

Tear a small piece off your paper, and write on it what you're thankful for. Then put it in your "jar." Keep adding papers until your jar is full.

Allow time for kids to express their thanks to God.

Say: **God gave the widow enough oil to fill every jar. And God has given us enough to fill *our* jars. Let's thank God for giving us what we need. I'll say a sentence in our prayer, and you'll respond to each line with "Thank you, God!"**

You give us food to eat. *(Thank you, God!)*

You give us clothes to wear. *(Thank you, God!)*

You give us beds to sleep in. *(Thank you, God!)*

You give us family and friends. *(Thank you, God!)*

You give us confidence. *(Thank you, God!)*

You give us strength. *(Thank you, God!)*

Thank you for always giving us what we need. Please use us to help others. Thank you for your amazing love. In Jesus' name, amen.

Encourage kids to take their "thankful" jars home to remind them to thank God for giving them what they need. Also encourage them to be on the lookout for ways God can use them to provide for others. As kids leave, remind them that <u>God gives us what we need</u>!

BIBLE STORY: **David praises God.** *(Psalm 23)*

BIBLE POINT: **God is loving.**

BIBLE VERSE: **"Surely your goodness and unfailing love will pursue me all the days of my life, and I will live in the house of the Lord forever"** *(Psalm 23:6).*

Bible Insight

▸ Psalm 23 has been called the most well-known psalm in the Bible. In the United States, its popularity may have been sparked by 19th-century preacher Henry Ward Beecher. In 1858, Beecher described Psalm 23 as "the nightingale of the psalms." Emphasizing God's love and compassion for us, the psalm is often read at funerals. In fact, by 1916 the Methodist church included Psalm 23 in the standard funeral litany. The King James version and other translations use the phrase "the valley of the shadow of death." But many modern translations use instead "dark valley" or "darkest valley." So in some modern translations, death is never mentioned in the psalm.

▸ The image of God as our shepherd is a common theme throughout the Bible. It first appears as early as in the book of Genesis (Genesis 48:15), where Jacob blesses Joseph's sons. The image appears elsewhere in the book of Psalms, as well as in the books of 2 Samuel, Micah, Ezekiel, and Isaiah. In the New Testament, Jesus himself is called our shepherd, most notably in the books of John and Hebrews.

▸ David begins Psalm 23 by calling to mind the pastoral life of a shepherd. Since David had been a shepherd, one might be inclined to think he wrote the psalm while watching his sheep and reflecting on God. However, many Bible scholars believe that David wrote this psalm when he was a much older man, many years after becoming king of Israel. Some even speculate that David wrote this psalm during the time his forces were battling those of his son Absalom. Looked at from that vantage point, Psalm 23 is a remarkable testament of the complete faith David had in his loving and compassionate God.

Kid Insight

Kids find out, often at a tender age, that love can be fleeting. Friends can be BFFs one day and not speaking the next. Parents divorce. Promises are broken. And kids themselves can be the ones who let others down. They realize that we're all human. We're all broken. But how wonderful to discover that we have a God who *isn't* broken! A God who will never leave us or disappoint us. Who will never turn his back on us or break a promise. Not only do we have a God who is loving, but we have a God who *is* love! What a privilege it is to help kids nurture a friendship with this incredible God who cares for us tenderly, like a shepherd cares for his sheep.

You'll need:

- ☐ kid-friendly Bible
- ☐ volunteer to play David
- ☐ Bible-times costume for David
- ☐ paper (1 sheet for every 4 kids)
- ☐ large paper clips (1 per child)
- ☐ craft sticks (1 per child)
- ☐ transparent tape (1 roll for every 4 kids)
- ☐ small balls (about 8)
- ☐ large sheets of poster board (1 for every 4 kids, plus 1 for you)
- ☐ black markers
- ☐ ping-pong balls (1 for every 4 kids)
- ☐ scissors
- ☐ cotton fabric (various colors)
- ☐ duct tape (various colors)
- ☐ elastic string
- ☐ colored markers
- ☐ chenille wires (1 per child)
- ☐ *Friends With God Bible Lessons Music* CD and music player

> If you can't find a volunteer to play David, modify your script slightly and play the role yourself. You'll simply need to have kids close their eyes and put on their imaginations while *you* don the Bible-times costume. If you're female, tweak the script and play this as a friend of David.

Getting Ready

Use a black marker to draw a fun squiggly path on a sheet of poster board with "Start" and "Finish" points similar to the drawing.

Make a sample Peaceful Rest Mask to show kids.

❧ THE LESSON ❧

Friend-Maker Icebreaker *(10 minutes)*

TOWER POWER

Welcome kids and introduce yourself.

Say: **Welcome! I'm glad you're here! To get started, I have a challenge for you.** Have kids form groups of four, and give each group a sheet of paper, four large paper clips, four craft sticks, and a roll of transparent tape. Say: **The challenge is to build the highest tower you can with the items you've been given. Each group has the same building materials. You can tear your paper, but no scissors will be provided. One last thing: Everyone needs to participate. You each have something to offer, so work together! You'll have six minutes...starting now!**

Give kids about six minutes to work on their towers. Play "God Loves Us So" from the *Friends With God Bible Lessons Music* CD softly in the background as kids play.

After about six minutes, turn off the music and call time. Have each group present its tower, and encourage kids from the other groups to give a round of applause for each presentation. Then compare the tower heights and declare the tallest. Ask:

💬 **How did working together help your group accomplish its goal?**

💬 **What was the hardest part of this activity?**

Say: **I gave you a lot of limitations in this activity! In a funny way, this reminds me of how we're limited in real life. We don't always have the right tools or talents for a particular job. But God is *never* limited, especially when it comes to love. God's love never fails—and I'm not making that up. It comes from the Bible!** Read aloud Psalm 36:5.

It just so happens that the psalm I just read was written by a guy named David—a pretty important person in the Bible. Let's meet David, because he knew for *certain* that <u>God is loving</u>.

Collect the towers and building supplies, and set them aside.

MEET DAVID

Place the small balls nearby. "David" should enter and begin a dialogue with kids. You may be needed to assist with props or lighting. Join in the fun and surprise of talking with this friend of God!

(Enters and talks with kids in a friendly manner.)

Hi! David here—nice to meet you! I heard that today you're discovering that God is loving. Boy, that's an understatement! If there's one thing I've learned throughout my life, it's that God loves me. He loved me when I was just a young shepherd boy, and he loved me when I was running for my life from a mean king. He loved me when I later BECAME king! He loved me when I was happy. When I was sad. Even when I was angry. God always loved me—and he loves you, too!

I overheard your teacher just now reading one of my psalms. I wrote a lot of psalms, you know. There's one of my favorites that kind of sums up how I feel about God. I'd like to share it with you, if that's okay. Here goes!

God is just like a shepherd, and I'm just like his sheep.

And I should know, since I used to be a shepherd! *Ask:*

💬 What IS a shepherd, anyhow? What does a shepherd do? *(Let kids call out answers.)*

A shepherd takes care of his sheep and protects them from harm. It's kind of like this. *(Have the leader place a handful of small balls on the floor in the center of the room. Appoint half the kids as shepherds to guard the sheep. Appoint the other kids as wild animals trying to attack the sheep. The shepherds can make a circle around the sheep, facing out. The wild animals will try to dart though the circle and grab the sheep while shepherds try to block them. Have the leader count to three and start play. Encourage the wild animals to make animal sounds. After about a minute, call time and have kids switch roles and play again. Then have everyone sit.) Ask:*

💬 Which role did you enjoy more, and why? *(Let kids call out answers.)*

💬 What would you have enjoyed least about being a shepherd back in my time? *(Let kids call out answers.)*

Yeah, it wasn't the most glamorous job, but it was an important job. Okay, let's move on—here's the next part of my psalm:

God gives me what I need and takes me to all the best places, like green fields and peaceful streams.

Do me a favor. Lie down on your back as if you were in a nice, green field next to a nice, cool stream. *(Pause as kids lie on their backs.)* Close your eyes for just a minute and imagine how peaceful that would be. *(Pause as kids close their eyes.)* Imagine a soft breeze and a few birds singing. So nice. So peaceful. God loves us so much that he can give us that kind of peace, right in the middle of our busy lives. The next line of my psalm goes like this:

God makes me strong and points me in the right direction.

(Choose one child to stand, and have the leader stand right next to the child.) Close your eyes and spin around in a circle three times. Your teacher will be right next to you in case you get dizzy. *(Have the child close his or her eyes and spin around three times.)* Now open your eyes. How do you feel? A little dizzy, a little weak? That's how it is in life sometimes. We get ourselves all turned around and don't know which way to go. But God is always right there to make us strong and guide us. *(Have the leader guide the child back to a sitting position.)*

Now the next part of my psalm gets a little more serious. Here's what I wrote:

God stays by my side so I'm never afraid when things get scary.

God keeps me safe and sound.

God takes care of me when others want to hurt me.

I don't know about you, but there have been plenty of times in my life when I've been in scary situations. Trust me—it's not all that pleasant to have an angry king chasing you around the countryside trying to kill you. *Ask:*

💬 **When is a time you were in a scary situation—a time you were afraid?** *(Have kids form pairs to discuss the question. Allow time, then ask a few willing kids to share their answers with the large group.)*

We all go through scary times. That's why I'm so thankful that God is loving. God loves us so much that he's always with us—to take care of us and protect us. God is so good to us!

Which is pretty much how I ended my psalm. Here's what I said:

God blesses me so much more than I deserve.

God's love will go with me wherever I go, for the rest of my life.

So there you have it. But there really aren't enough words in the whole world to describe how I feel about God. I love him so much. But he loves me a million times more. He loves YOU that way, too!

Being one of God's sheep is awesome, isn't it? I can't imagine anything better. God does it all! God is stronger, wiser, and bigger than anything or anyone that might come our way.

Well, thanks for listening to my psalm! Hope you liked it. I wrote lots of psalms, you know, so you can read them in the Bible any time you want! 'Bye!

(Wave to kids and exit.)

BETWEEN THE LINES

Say: **In Psalm 23, David's words are about God guiding and watching over us like a shepherd guides and watches over his sheep.**

Let's play a fun game where you'll try to guide a ball along a path to the finish line. You'll watch over the ball, trying to keep it on the path and prevent it from falling to the ground.

Form teams of four players. Give each team a sheet of poster board, a ping-pong ball, and a black marker. Have kids draw a wandering path with start and finish points. Encourage kids to add a stream, a field, and some sheep looking a little scared. Show kids your example for inspiration. For extra fun, let kids draw a face on the ping-pong ball.

Have players stand and hold on to the corners of the poster board. Explain that teammates will work together to roll the ball from start to finish while keeping the ball inside the path. Everyone will keep a close eye on the ball, and when it rolls away from the path, they'll call "out of bounds" and then work together to get the ball back on the path.

Teams can work with the same board for a few rounds until they feel like they've done well keeping the ball on the path from start to finish. Then let kids switch game boards with other teams to take on new challenges as long as time allows.

Play "God Loves Us So" from the *Friends With God Bible Lessons Music* CD softly in the background as kids play.

Then collect the supplies and have kids sit with their teams. Ask:

💬 **How well were you able to watch over your ball?**

💬 **What are some ways God guides and watches over you?** Share an example of your own to help kids get started. For example, maybe God led you to a song or Bible verse that was just what you needed to hear during a difficult time.

Say: <u>God is loving</u>. **He's our shepherd who watches over us and guides us on the path of life. He brings us to peaceful places and sticks with us when life gets scary.**

PEACEFUL REST MASKS

Say: **Let's make something to remind us of David's psalm in the Bible. Our craft can help us remember that <u>God is loving</u>. But first let me ask you something.** Ask:

💬 **Would you rather go to bed early and get up early or go to bed late and sleep in? Why?**

💬 **Do you usually sleep peacefully or wake up a lot in the night?**

Say: **We're going to make a craft called a Peaceful Rest Mask that can remind us that <u>God is loving</u>. Because God loves us so much, we can rest easy at night! Let's get creative!**

Set out paper, colored markers, poster board, scissors, cotton fabric, duct tape, and elastic string for kids to share. Have kids follow these easy instructions to make sleep masks.

▸ **Draw a sleep mask shape on a piece of paper, then cut it out.**

▸ **Trace it onto a piece of poster board, and then cut it out.**

▸ **Use the poster board pattern to trace the mask twice onto the fabric of your choice.**

▸ **Cut out the fabric.**

▸ **Use duct tape around the edges to attach the fabric to both sides of the poster board.**

▸ **Pinch one side of the mask, and then cut a small slit where you've pinched it. Repeat on the other side.**

▸ **Cut a length of elastic string that fits snugly around your head. Tie the elastic string through each slit in the mask.**

▸ **Use markers to decorate the fabric on the outside of the sleep mask. You may want to write the Bible point: <u>God is loving</u>.**

When kids have finished, let them show off their masks to each other. Then ask:

💬 **What are some things you worry about that might keep you awake at night?**

💬 **How can you trust God with those worries?**

Say: <u>**God is loving**</u>. **The Bible says he lets us rest in green meadows and lie beside peaceful streams. God takes care of us like a shepherd takes care of his sheep. When we trust God to watch over us, we can rest easy. We don't need to always be alert or worrying. We can put on our sleep masks and rest in God's peace.**

Have kids take their sleep masks home and tell their friends and families that <u>God is loving</u> and cares for us so we can rest easy.

Let kids help put away the supplies and clean up.

A Loving Shepherd

Have kids sit in a circle on the floor. Say: **Today we talked more about God, and we discovered that** <u>**God is loving**</u>**. He watches over us and cares for us like a shepherd cares for his sheep.** Bend a chenille wire into a shepherd's staff—it should look like the shape of a candy cane. Hold it up for kids to see. Say: **To remind us of God,** *our* **shepherd, let's make shepherds' staffs.**

A shepherd's staff is used to guide sheep if they go off course. If a sheep goes somewhere it shouldn't or maybe gets stuck, the shepherd can put the hook part around the sheep and pull it to safety. God watches over us like a shepherd and guides us to safety and peace. Give each child a chenille wire, and have kids shape the wires into shepherds' staffs.

Let's think about what a shepherd actually does and see how that applies to God being our shepherd. Hold your shepherd's staff in front of you and picture a shepherd out in a field, watching over his flock of sheep. Ask:

💬 **What kinds of things does a shepherd do for his sheep?**

Let kids call out answers, such as feeding the sheep, making sure they have water, giving them rest, making sure none wander off, helping any that get hurt, and protecting them from wild animals. For each answer kids offer, compare that to God being a shepherd by saying things like "God protects us, too" and "God provides for us, too."

Then say: <u>**God is loving**</u>**, and he cares for us just like a shepherd. Now use your chenille wire to make the shape of a heart.** Pause. **Hold the heart between your hands as I thank God for loving us.**

Pray: **God, thank you for letting us be your sheep. Thank you for watching over us and caring for us like a good shepherd. Thank you for guiding us and giving us rest and peace. Thank you for being with us when times are scary. And most of all, thank you so much for loving us! In Jesus' name, amen.**

Encourage kids to take their chenille wire hearts and Peaceful Rest Masks home to remind them that <u>**God is loving**</u>**.**

ALL FIRED UP

BIBLE STORY: **Shadrach, Meshach, and Abednego and the fiery furnace.** *(Daniel 3)*

BIBLE POINT: <u>**God helps us do what's right.**</u>

BIBLE VERSE: **"Trust in the Lord with all your heart; do not depend on your own understanding. Seek his will in all you do, and he will show you which path to take"** *(Proverbs 3:5-6).*

Bible Insight

▸ The fiery furnace in Daniel 3 was likely a kiln or similar high-heat oven. Kilns are often wood-burning chambers that can be heated to scorching temperatures for hardening clay into pottery. Some modern kilns can reach temperatures well beyond 2,000 degrees Fahrenheit. That's in the realm of the typical temperature of molten lava found in volcanoes! If the fiery furnace, heated seven times hotter, approached that kind of temperature, it's no wonder it killed the soldiers guarding Shadrach, Meshach, and Abednego.

▸ Environmental or air temperature around 130 degrees Fahrenheit will bring on dangerous, very possibly fatal heat stroke. The temperature inside the fiery furnace could have been beyond 2,000 degrees. There's no scientific phenomenon that explains how Shadrach, Meshach, and Abednego walked around inside the furnace without quickly being reduced to ashes—and that they emerged without so much as a singed eyebrow.

▸ Shadrach, Meshach, and Abednego hailed from the tribe of Judah and had Hebrew names. Hananiah became Shadrach, Mishael's name changed to Meshach, and Azariah acquired the name Abednego. Their Babylonian captors changed their names (and Daniel's, too) when the young men began training to serve in King Nebuchadnezzar's royal palace.

▸ Of all the young men chosen from the tribe of Judah to enter training for royal service, none impressed King Nebuchadnezzar as much as Daniel, Hananiah (Shadrach), Mishael (Meshach), and Azariah (Abednego). Yet after the king had decreed everyone must bow to his golden statue and the young men refused because of their faith in the one true God, Nebuchadnezzar quickly turned on them. Standing up to a dangerously fickle king such as Nebuchadnezzar further shows the steadfast faith in God that brought courage to Shadrach, Meshach, and Abednego.

Kid Insight

Part of childhood is learning to navigate right and wrong. Through trial and error, rewards and consequences, observing influencers, and more, kids develop a sense for what's right and how to act accordingly. Unfortunately, *knowing* the right thing to do doesn't always make it easy to *do* it! No wonder Paul lamented about human nature when he wrote in Romans 7:15, "I don't really understand myself, for I want to do what is right, but I don't do it. Instead, I do what I hate."

How refreshing it is to discover that we can fully rely on God, who not only *knows* what's right but also helps us *do* what's right. It's vital for kids to know that God isn't leaving them to do it all on their own, just as God didn't leave Shadrach, Meshach, and Abednego to stand up for him alone. God gave them the courage to boldly stand up for God and even intervened in the fiery furnace. That same God is ready to engage with kids, talk with them, and equip them to do what's right. Even when it's really, really hard.

You'll need:

- ☐ kid-friendly Bible
- ☐ volunteer to play Shadrach
- ☐ volunteer to play an angel
- ☐ Bible-times costume for Shadrach
- ☐ white robe or bedsheet for the angel to wear
- ☐ red, orange, and yellow crepe paper cut to 5-foot lengths (3 or 4 strips of each color)
- ☐ flicker lights (1 per child, plus 1 for Shadrach)
- ☐ *Friends With God Bible Lessons Music* CD and music player
- ☐ red string or lacing cord cut to 8-inch lengths (1 length per child)
- ☐ orange string or lacing cord cut to 8-inch lengths (1 length per child)
- ☐ yellow string or lacing cord cut to 8-inch lengths (1 length per child)
- ☐ scissors

> If you can't find a volunteer to play Shadrach, modify your script slightly and play the role yourself. You'll simply need to have kids close their eyes and put on their imaginations while *you* don the Bible-times costume. If you're female, tweak the script and play this as a palace worker who heard the incredible story. If you can't find someone to play the angel, connect with a child ahead of time and have him or her wear the "angel" costume and play the role.

Getting Ready

Make a set of one red, one orange, and one yellow string for each child. Tie each set of strings together at one end with a knot. Leave a 1-inch "tail" above the knot.

~❧ THE LESSON ❧~

Friend-Maker Icebreaker *(10 minutes)*

CHALLENGING CHOICES

Welcome kids and introduce yourself.

Say: **I'm glad you're here today! Whether it was your choice to be here or someone else's, it was a good choice that brought you here. Our days are full of choices. Think about how many choices you made even just this morning in getting ready for the day. You chose what to wear, what to have for breakfast, what to say to the first person you saw in the morning—you can lose count quickly!**

Let's dive in to our time together with a fun way to make some choices. As we play, try to remember which choices are easy for you to make and which are harder.

Gather everyone in the center of the room, and explain that for each "would you rather" situation you give, kids will vote for their answers by running to the side of the room you designate for each choice.

Call out the following scenarios, allowing time in between for kids to move to opposite ends of the room to cast their votes and then come back to the center near you.

Say: **Would you rather...**

- 💬 **brush your teeth every day to keep them healthy or never brush and live with painful cavities?**
- 💬 **eat only pizza or only tacos for a whole week?**
- 💬 **spend $100 on one really cool thing you want or split it up to buy a few fun things?**
- 💬 **take a test after studying or take a test without studying at all?**
- 💬 **scuba dive with sharks or giant whales?**
- 💬 **spend an entire day playing outside or playing video games?**
- 💬 **be known for being generous or funny?**
- 💬 **vacation in mountains or at a beach?**
- 💬 **win a trip to Disney World or a trip on a rocket to see Earth from space?**
- 💬 **show up to a friend's birthday party early or late?**
- 💬 **have a superpower to fly or travel through time?**
- 💬 **be able to sing *really* well or play a sport *really* well?**

Gather kids in the center of the room.

Say: **Some of those choices were fun and even silly, and some were harder to make.** Ask:

- 💬 **Which choices were hardest for you to make, and why?**
- 💬 **What's a hard choice you've had to make recently? How did you decide what to do?**

Share your own example first, such as choosing to take a job (or leave a job) or what color to paint your house. Then let kids share with a few kids sitting nearby so everyone has a chance to talk. Then draw attention back to yourself.

Say: **It can be hard to do what's right when the right thing isn't a clear choice. Or sometimes we *do* know what's right but we also know that doing it will be really hard—even scary. Three guys in the Bible faced a difficult, scary decision, but their amazing story shows us that even when it's hard, <u>God helps us do what's right</u>. Let's meet one of those friends now!**

MEET SHADRACH

Place the flicker lights nearby. "Shadrach" should enter and begin a dialogue with kids. You may be needed to assist with props or lighting effects. Join in the fun and surprise of bringing this amazing story to life!

(Put a flicker light in your pocket. Then enter smiling.)

That looked like a fun game of choices! It made me think about a time I and a couple of other guys faced a really big choice. Oh! *(Hit your forehead with the heel of your hand and roll your eyes.)* I forgot to introduce myself! I'm Shadrach. I know, I know, it's a unique name. But my friends are Meshach and Abednego—that last one's a mouthful! *(Give a lighthearted laugh.)*

Anyway, you know those times EVERYBODY is doing something popular—except you? Maybe that just happened for you in the game. Or maybe it has happened at school. *Ask:*

💬 When have you felt pressure to make a choice because it's what everyone else was doing?
  (Let a few kids share their responses with the group, then continue.)

Well, my two friends and I know what that's like. King Nebuchadnezzar had built this giant golden statue of himself *(stand up as tall as possible)*, and he demanded that everyone bow down to it. Seriously, it was huge: 90 feet tall! Whenever the king's music played, Nebuchadnezzar wanted every single person to stop what he or she was doing and worship his idol.

(Shake your head "no" with a stern face.)

But not Meshach, Abednego, and I. We worship God—and ONLY God. We stood strong and stood by our God—and this also meant we stood out from the crowd. The king's advisers definitely noticed we weren't doing what we were told. Here, I'll give you an idea of what it was like to stand strong under pressure.

(Have kids find partners of similar size. Have partners stand facing each other, toe to toe, and then have one person step slightly to the side. Next, partners will press the sides of their closest feet against each other and hold hands with their closest hands.)

You'll use your arm strength to try to pull your partner off balance while he or she is trying to do the same to you. Do your best to stand strong!

(Cue kids to start working against their partners while trying to stand strong themselves. After partners play a few rounds, have everyone switch partners to play again—still pairing up with others of fairly equal size. Then have everyone sit around you.) Ask:

💬 What was it like to stand strong when someone was trying to force you to do something?

Standing strong isn't easy. It got even worse for me and my two friends! King Nebuchadnezzar got super upset when he heard we refused his command. He ordered us into his throne room and gave us one more chance to bow to his golden statue. If we refused again, he would throw us into his fiery furnace. Where I live, a furnace was like a whole room for fire! They used it to melt metal to make things like…well, statues! It was hotter than hot! Rub your hands together as fast as you can for as long as you can to feel how hot that can get.

(Pause and let kids rub their hands together until they can feel heat. They can also heat up their hands and touch the person next to them on the arm to see whose hands got hotter.)

Now try to imagine heat THOUSANDS of times hotter than that. Scorching, burning heat that no human could survive. That's what we were facing if we didn't do what Nebuchadnezzar ordered us to do. Even then, we said "Never!" It was a tough choice…because we knew we could *(gulp)* die. But we love God, and he helped us do the right thing.

The king boiled with rage. *(Jump up and down as if you're mad.)* **He ordered his furnace to be made** *(hold up seven fingers)* **seven times hotter than usual. Then he screamed,** *(use a big, angry voice)* **"THROW THEM IN!" The fire was so hot that it even killed the guards who tossed us in.**

(Cue the leader to run around the kids, wildly waving the fire-colored crepe paper streamers above and around them. The angel should also slip into the room and hide somewhere nearby so he or she can sneak up to the kids.)

The flames swirled and flashed all around us. But we kept our cool.

(Have kids try to keep straight faces and not flinch at all while the leader continues to wildly wave and whip the streamers near them for about a minute.)

We knew God could save us. And even if he didn't, we knew we'd done the right thing.

(Cue the leader to stop waving the streamers and set them aside. As you continue, the angel can sneak up and quietly sit behind the kids.)

When Nebuchadnezzar looked inside the furnace *(hold your hands flat at your eyebrows and squint like you're straining to peer into the glowing furnace, and have the kids do the same)*, **he couldn't believe what he saw. Not only were we still alive, but there was also a FOURTH man standing with us. We weren't in there alone!**

(Draw attention to the angel who has carefully, quietly sat near the kids. The angel smiles warmly and waves.)

God had sent an angel to stand by our side!

The king called us out of the furnace. We stepped out of the fire *(step forward as if out of the furnace)* **without a single hair on our heads singed or a thread on our clothes scorched. We didn't even smell like smoke.** *(Smell the collar of your top.)* **Nope, not one little bit.**

(The angel can sneak away quietly.)

Nebuchadnezzar had no choice. After what he had just seen, he HAD to praise our God. Now the king's heart was on fire for the one true God. He cried out, "Praise the God of Shadrach, Meshach, and Abednego!"

The king was so impressed that he actually gave us even MORE important jobs in his kingdom. And our love for God burned as bright as ever. *(Pull the flicker light out of your pocket and turn it on.)*

Some might say our story is one about three guys, but we know better. This is a story about FOUR because God was with us the whole time. God's here now, too, even when we can't SEE him. It won't always be easy to take a stand for what we know is right, but God is with us, and <u>God helps us do what's right</u>!

(Cue the leader to give a flicker light to each child, and have kids turn on the flicker lights.)

I want you all to keep these flames as a reminder of how God saved me and my friends from the fire and how we can let our love for God shine bright in doing the right thing and sticking with God no matter what. Stand strong and shine bright!

(Wave goodbye and exit.)

WHEN THE RIGHT WAY'S THE HARD WAY

Say: <u>God helps us do what's right</u>, just as he helped Shadrach and his friends. God gave Shadrach, Meshach, and Abednego courage to do the right thing. They were brave when it seemed like there was no way they'd get through such a mess.

Let's play a game where you'll face getting through a challenge that gets harder and harder, but in a fun way!

Invite three willing kids to be the first King's Advisers, who'll be trying to tag and trap everyone else. Have the King's Advisers stand in a line in the center of the room, with all the other kids on one side facing the King's Advisers. The goal is for everyone to get past the King's Advisers without getting tagged. The King's Advisers can't move from where they stand, but they can turn to face different directions and lean to reach with their arms to tag others as they run by.

Anyone who's tagged becomes a King's Adviser and stands in the line. Everyone who gets through to the other side will continue to run from one side of the room to the other while trying to avoid getting tagged. The challenge should increase with each round as more King's Advisers are added.

When everyone has been tagged, end the round and choose three new King's Advisers. Play "Through It All" from the *Friends With God Bible Lessons Music* CD while kids play as many rounds as time allows. Then gather everyone to sit around you. Ask:

💬 **What was it like to run through the King's Adviser line as it filled with more people?**

💬 **What could've helped you get through the line of people?**

Say: **In the game, getting through the King's Advisers got difficult! In real life, it can be hard to get through things like tough homework assignments, arguments with your family, or friends who don't get along. When we face those challenges, usually there are right ways to respond and wrong ways to respond.**

Give your own example of a hard time and the choices you faced in that challenge. For example, maybe you had a fight with your spouse and you know the *right* thing to do is apologize. Or perhaps you had a hard project at work and you know the *right* thing to do is stay later to get the project done. Ask:

💬 **Think of a challenge you've faced recently. What was the right way to get through that hard time?**

Say: **God doesn't leave us alone when we have a hard decision to make or are facing something that's just not easy! Keep that challenge you just thought of in your mind as you listen to these words from the Bible.** Read aloud Proverbs 3:5-6. Ask:

💬 **How do you feel about that challenge when you hear this verse? Why?**

Say: **The Bible is full of encouragement that helps us stand strong and do things God's way. When we trust God, *he* will show us the right way to go. <u>God helps us do what's right</u>.**

FRIENDS IN THE FIRE WRISTBANDS

Set out the sets of string or lacing you cut beforehand.

Say: **The three friends could trust in God and rely on him to help them do what was right. But they also had each other! One way <u>God helps us do what's right</u> is by surrounding us with friends and family members who guide our choices. Listen to how the Bible puts it.** Read aloud Ecclesiastes 4:12. Ask:

🗩 **How can having friends by your side help you stay strong in doing what's right?**

🗩 **Who are some friends or family members who help you do what's right?**

Say: **Let's make some friendship wristbands that remind us of the way <u>God helps us do what's right</u>, and let's thank God for the friends he puts in our lives.**

Invite a willing child to help you demonstrate how to make a friendship wristband by braiding the strings together in a classic braid. Have your partner hold the end of the strings with the knot so you can work with the free ends to braid. You may need to demonstrate how to braid a few times for kids who have never braided. Once you've braided the strings to where there's about an inch of the strings left free, tie another knot to secure the braid and complete the wristband.

Have everyone grab a set of strings and find a partner. Then partners can take turns holding the knotted end of each other's wristbands while the other partner braids. If one partner is better at braiding, he or she can coach and encourage his or her partner in braiding.

When everyone has finished, gather kids around you, holding their wristbands so they can look at them.

Say: **Not only did Shadrach, Meshach, and Abednego have an amazing friend in God, but God didn't make them face the fire alone. The friends didn't just have God's power with them, they also had each other. Having friends who'll choose to do what's right with us can make a huge difference.**

You can keep your wristband and wear it to remind you to surround yourself with friends who'll do what's right and to remind you that your truest, most powerful friend—God—is always with you. Or you can give the wristband to a friend or family member and tell all about what this cord of three strands means.

THE LIGHT TO DO WHAT'S RIGHT

Have everyone stand in a circle. Kids can tuck their wristbands in their pockets if they haven't tied them on their wrists. Have kids hold their unlit flicker lights Shadrach gave them after telling his story.

Say: <u>God helps us do what's right</u>. **When we try to stand up for what's right using only our own strength, it can be hard. Stand on one foot.** Pause. **While you do, talk with God about an area of your life where you need help standing strong. Maybe your friends try to get you to make fun of other kids. Maybe your neighbors tell jokes you know God wouldn't like, but you're tempted to go along with them. Ask God for help to shine his light and do what's right. When you've finished praying, put your foot down and stand firmly. Then you can turn on your light and hold it out, trusting that God is going to help you do what's right.**

Allow time for silent prayer until all the kids are back on two feet.

Pray: **God, you help us do what's right. On our own, we won't always make the right choices. But you'll help us be strong like Shadrach, Meshach, and Abednego. Thank you for your help! In Jesus' name, amen.**

Let kids take their flicker lights home along with their wristbands as reminders that God will help them shine his light in doing what's right.